항공
객실서비스
영어

Cengage

Airline Cabin Service English

Lee Hyo Seon
Lee Jin Young

ISBN-13: 978-89-6218-554-6

Cengage Learning Korea Ltd.
14F YTN Newsquare 76 Sangamsan-ro
Mapo-gu Seoul 03926 Korea

Printed in Korea
Print Number: 01 Print Year: 2023

Airline Cabin Service English

항공 객실서비스 영어

이효선 · 이진영 지음

Cengage

Australia • Brazil • Canada • Mexico • Singapore • United Kingdom • United States

항공 객실서비스 영어

초판 1쇄 인쇄 2023년 10월 12일
초판 1쇄 발행 2023년 10월 19일
지은이 이효선, 이진영
발행인 송성헌
편집기획 김민정
발행처 센게이지러닝코리아(주)
등록번호 제313-2007-000074호(2007.3.19)
주소 서울시 마포구 상암산로 76 YTN 뉴스퀘어 14층
이메일 asia.infokorea@cengage.com
홈페이지 www.cengage.co.kr
ISBN-13 978-89-6218-554-6

정가 23,000원

Preface

이 책은 항공사 객실 승무원이 되기 위해 공부하는 분들을 위한 실무 영어 지침서입니다. 승객의 항공기 탑승에서부터 하기 시까지의 서비스 순서별 다양한 상황을 대화식으로 풀어내어 쉽게 상황을 이해할 수 있도록 하였으며, 자주 사용하는 상용구들의 반복 학습을 통해 실제 상황에 적용하기 쉽도록 구성하였습니다.

각 장은 Words and Phrases, Useful Expressions, Conversation, Phrases Tips, Activity로 구성되어 있습니다. 먼저 각 장에서 많이 사용하게 될 단어와 문장을 익히고, 상용구와 함께 상황별 대화를 학습합니다. 그리고 동일한 의미를 나타내는 다양한 표현 방법을 익힘으로써 학습자들이 보다 많은 어휘를 구사할 수 있게 하였습니다. 또한 학습한 내용에 대해 연습문제를 풀어 봄으로써 자신의 학습 정도를 점검할 수 있게 하였습니다. 마지막으로, 이 책의 가장 주목할 부분으로 Reading Comprehension은 항공 산업과 관련된 다양한 내용을 수록함으로써 항공산업 전반에 대한 이해를 넓히고 동시에 이를 영어로 학습할 수 있는 기회를 제공하고자 하였습니다.

이 책은 지금 이 순간에도 항공사 객실 승무원이 되고자 노력하는 모든 분에게 항공 산업의 전반적인 지식과 객실에서의 다양한 상황을 익히고, 그에 맞는 영어 대화를 학습하는 데 커다란 도움을 드릴 수 있으리라 생각합니다. 이 책과 함께하는 모든 분이 푸른 창공을 향해 멋진 날개를 펼치게 되길 진심으로 응원합니다.

저자 일동

Contents

PART 3

PART 4

PART 5

PART

1

Boarding & Ground Service

UNIT 1

Greeting & Boarding

Words and Phrases

Match the words with the sentences.

cabin　lavatory　flight　welcome　aisle
take　aboard　in the back

1. Your seat is ________________ of the cabin.

2. _________ _________ . May I see your boarding pass, please?

3. You may go down the _________ on your left.

4. Your seat number is 45H. Please _________ the other aisle.

5. You can use the __________ in the middle of the cabin.

6. I hope you enjoy the _________ .

7. Your seat is in the next section of the __________ .

Useful Expressions

1. Good morning(afternoon, evening). Welcome aboard.
2. Excuse me. May I see your boarding pass, please?
3. We are rechecking your boarding pass for security reason.
4. Please take the other aisle.
5. Your seat is in the middle of the cabin.
6. Your seat is a window seat.
7. Please go right down this aisle.
8. Please go through here, and all the way back.
9. Please proceed the other aisle.
10. Thank you for your cooperation.
11. Would you please step aside for the other passengers?

Conversation

Read the dialogues below and practice speaking with your partner by taking turns.

Dialogue 1_ Boarding pass check at the boarding gate

F/A : Good morning, sir. Welcome aboard.[1] May I see your boarding pass, please?[2]
PAX : Good morning? Here's my boarding pass.
F/A : Thank you. This way, please. Your seat is in the middle of the cabin, on your right.
PAX : Thank you.
F/A : My pleasure. Have a nice flight.

Alternative Expressions

1. I'm pleased to have you on board today. It's nice/good to have you on board.
2. Let me see your boarding pass. Would you show me your boarding pass, please?

Dialogue 2_ Boarding pass check at the boarding gate

F/A : Good evening, ma'am. Welcome aboard. May I see your boarding pass, please?
PAX : I know where my seat is. My seat number is 18B.
F/A : I'm sorry, ma'am, but we have to recheck the boarding pass individually for security.
PAX : OK. Here's my boarding pass.
F/A : Thank you for your cooperation. Your seat is in the front of the cabin, on your right side.

Dialogue 3_ Seating guide in the cabin

PAX : Excuse me, Miss. My seat is 23C. Which one is my seat?
F/A : Your seat is an aisle seat. Right here, ma'am.
PAX : Oh, thanks.
F/A : No problem.

Dialogue 4_ Seating guide in the cabin

F/A : Excuse me, sir. Would you please step aside to let these people through?
PAX : Oh, I'm sorry.
F/A : That's okey, sir. Thank you.

Dialogue 5_ Seating guide in the cabin

F/A : Excuse me, ma'am. Would you please take your seat during boarding?
We have to keep the aisle open during boarding.
PAX : Oh, I see.
F/A : Thank you for your understanding, ma'am.

Dialogue 6_ Seating guide in the cabin

PAX : Excuse me, Miss. Could you help me to find my seat?
F/A : Certainly, sir. What's your seat number?
PAX : 53K.
F/A : Come this way, please. Your seat is in the back of the cabin.
Right here, sir. It's a window seat.
PAX : Thank you.
F/A : My pleasure.[1]

Alternative Expressions

1. You're welcome. Not at all. Don't mention it. I'm happy to help.

Phrases Tips

다음 구문을 활용해 다양한 문장을 만들어 보세요.

Your seat is in the	front middle back	of the cabin	on the right. on the left.

Please	take go down go through proceed to proceed down	this aisle. that aisle. the other aisle.

Activity

다음 대화를 완성하세요.

Time : 6:00 pm.
Place : boarding gate
Occasion : greeting passengers

F/A : ____

____?

PAX : I know where my seat is.

F/A : ____

____

PAX : O.K. Here's my boarding pass.

F/A : ____

____

Reading Comprehension

다음을 읽고 물음에 답하세요.

Greeting Passengers While Boarding

When boarding a plane, flight attendants perform various tasks. Among them, the most important role is to ensure the safety of passengers. Flight attendants are responsible for safely evacuating passengers in emergency situations, guiding them on safe evacuation methods, and informing them of the location of emergency exits.

In addition, flight attendants provide various services for the convenience of passengers. This includes providing drinks or snacks, cleaning the restroom, and providing portable baby beds. Flight attendants respond quickly to passengers' requests and do their best to ensure that passengers can enjoy their flight comfortably.

Furthermore, flight attendants also have the role of greeting passengers upon boarding. This is to greet passengers kindly and make them feel at ease so that they can enjoy their flight without worries.

Also, flight attendants are responsible for maintaining safety inside the airplane. This includes ensuring that items inside the airplane are well organized so that passengers can move safely inside the airplane, and that emergency exits are well marked.

Finally, flight attendants are also responsible for providing passengers with flight information. This includes informing passengers about the altitude, speed, and weather information of the airplane. Through this, passengers can understand the operational situation of the airplane and enjoy the flight with peace of mind.

1. 탑승 시 승무원의 역할은 무엇인가요?

2. 승무원들이 환영 인사를 하는 이유는 무엇인가요?

3. 승무원들이 제공하는 비행 정보는 어떤 것인가요?

UNIT 2

Baggage Handling

Words and Phrases

Match the words with the sentences.

belongings　　keep　　coatroom　　overhead bin

step aside　　take out

1. Would you like me to _______ your coat in the __________ ?

2. Please put your bag in the _____________ .

3. You can ____________ your bag after the altitude stabilizes after take-off.

4. Please ___________ to let others through.

5. Let me know if you need help with your ______________ .

Useful Expressions

1. Do you need help with your belongings?
2. Please put your bag in the overhead bin.
3. We have to keep the aisle clear during the flight.
4. Would you please put your baggage under the seat in front of you?
5. Storing your bag here is not allowed.

Space_Cat / iStock / Getty Images Plus

Conversation

Read the dialogues below and practice speaking with your partner by taking turns.

Dialogue 1_ Baggage securing

F/A : Good morning, ma'am. May I help with your bag?
PAX : Thank you.
F/A : I'll put your bag in the overhead compartment.
PAX : How nice of you. Thanks.
F/X : I'm happy to help you, sir.

Dialogue 2_ Baggage securing

PAX : Excuse, me. Could you help me put this bag in the overhead bin?
F/A : Sure.
......
I'm sorry, ma'am, but I am afraid your bag is too heavy to put in the overhead bin. Would you mind putting it under the seat in front of you?
PAX : Not at all.
F/A : Thank you for your understanding.

Dialogue 3_ Baggage securing

F/A : Excuse me, sir. Are these bags yours?
PAX : Yes. Why?
F/A : I am sorry, but we have to keep the aisle clear during the flight.
If you don't mind, I will put them in the overhead bin.
PAX : Oh, really? I'm sorry. I'll do it.
F/A : Let me help you, sir. Thank you for your cooperation.

Dialogue 4_ Baggage securing

F/A : Excuse me, ma'am. You should not put your bag on the other bag. It might fall down during turbulence.

PAX : OK. Then, where can I put my baggage?

F/A : Let me help you with that.
There's room in this overhead compartment.

PAX : Thanks a lot.

F/A : My pleasure.

ANNOUNCEMENT Baggage handling

Ladies and gentlemen, thank you for flying with us today.

This is __________ Air bound for ______________ .

For your safety, please place your carry-on items in the overhead bin or under the seat in front of you.

Thank you.

Phrases Tips

다음 구문을 활용해 다양한 문장을 만들어 보세요.

Would you please Would you like me to	keep put	your bag it	in the overhead bins. under the seat. in front of you.

We have to keep the aisle	clear open free	during the flight. at all times.

Activity

다음 문장을 이용하여 기내 대화를 만드세요.

1. Storing your bag here is not allowed.

2. We must keep the aisle clear.

3. Your bag is too heavy.

4. It might fall down during turbulence.

5. I'll keep your bag in the overhead bin just above your seat.

6. You can put it in this overhead compartment.

Reading Comprehension

다음을 읽고 물음에 답하세요.

Airline In-flight Baggage Regulations

The regulations for carry-on baggage on board vary depending on the seat class of the airline. Generally, they are classified into economy, business, and first class, and the size, weight, and quantity of carry-on baggage allowed for each class are different.

For economy class, most airlines allow free carry-on baggage that is less than or equal to 115cm in length, width, and height combined and weighs less than 10kg. However, some airlines may have stricter restrictions on weight or size, so it is important to check the airline's regulations.

For business and first class, more carry-on baggage is allowed than in economy class. Most airlines allow free carry-on baggage that is less than or equal to 115cm in length, width, and height combined and weighs less than 18kg. In addition, some airlines may allow additional personal items such as a personal bag or laptop bag. However, as regulations vary by airline, it is important to check the airline's regulations before traveling.

Also, safety accidents of in-flight baggage can occur for various reasons. For instance, baggage stored above the seats may have moved due to sudden movements of the plane. This can occur when the baggage is not properly secured or when the baggage compartment is not properly closed. Electronic devices, chargers, liquids, and others may be stored in the baggage, and may sometimes cause a fire due to overheating or from collisions.

To prevent these in-flight baggage safety accidents, it is important to store the baggage safely. Always make sure to close the baggage compartment properly and secure the baggage.

1. 좌석 등급별 기내 수하물 규정은 어떻게 되나요?

2. 추가로 허용되는 물품은 무엇인가요?

3. 기내 수하물 안전사고 발생 원인은 무엇인가요?

UNIT 3

Seating Arrangement

Words and Phrases

Match the words with the sentences.

mistake	appreciate	inconvenience
separately	apologize	rearranged

1. Your seat has been ______________ near the galley.

2. I ____________ it very much for switching seat with the passenger.

3. I'm sorry there was a ____________ in the seating arrangement.

4. I'm sorry for the _________________ .

5. My husband and I were seated ____________ .
   Can you change seats for us?

6. We ____________ for the confusion.

Useful Expressions

1. I'm sorry, but I'm afraid you are in the wrong seat.
2. Would you please wait here for a moment while I check it for you?
3. Would you please wait until everyone has boarded?
4. I'll guide you to your seat.
5. Could you please change your seat?
6. Your seat is right behind this seat.
7. I'm afraid there was a mistake in the seating arrangement.
8. Your seat has been rearranged.
9. I'll check if we have any empty seat available.
10. All the seats are occupied today.
11. We have some empty seats in the middle of the cabin.

Conversation

Read the dialogues below and practice speaking with your partner by taking turns.

Dialogue 1_ Seating in a wrong seat

PAX1 : Excuse me, Miss. There is someone in my seat.

F/A : I'll check it for you, sir. (to PAX2) Excuse me, sir. May I see your boarding pass, please? Thank you. I'm sorry, but I'm afraid you are in the wrong seat. Your seat is right behind this one.

PAX2 : Oh, I'm sorry.

PAX1 : That's OK.

F/A : Thank you for waiting, sir. Is there anything else that I can help you?

PAX1 : I'm fine. Thanks.

F/A : You're welcome.

Dialogue 2_ Separate seat

PAX : Excuse me, Miss. My wife and I are sitting in separate seats. If there are two empty seats next to each other, we would like to sit together. Would that be possible?

<case 1>

F/A : Just a moment, please. Let me check if there are empty seats.

......

We have some empty seats that you and your wife can sit together in the back of the cabin. Would that be alright?

PAX : Okay.

F/A : Please take your belongings and follow me. I'll guide you.

PAX : Thank you for your help.

F/A : It's my pleasure.

<case 2>

F/A : Wait a moment, please. I'll check it for you.

......

I am very sorry, sir. All the seats are occupied today.

PAX1 : Well, could you ask the passenger sitting next to my wife?

F/A : Certainly, sir. Where is your wife sitting?

PAX1 : 35A

F/A : Just a moment, please.

......

(to PAX2) Excuse me, ma'am. I'm sorry for disturbing you, but this lady sitting next to you and her husband are in separate seats. And they want to sit together. Would you mind changing seats?

PAX2 : Okay. Then where should I seat?

F/A : Thank you for your kind understanding. Please take your belongings and follow me.

......

(to PAX1) There's a good news, sir. This lady agreed to change seats with you. So you and your wife can sit together.

PAX1 : Thank you very much.

PAX2 : No problem.

F/A : It's my pleasure.

<case 3>

F/A : I'm very sorry, sir. I'm afraid I was unable to arrange seats for you and your wife.

PAX : That's fine.

F/A : Thank you for your kind understanding. If there is anything that you need during the flight, please let me know.

Dialogue 3_ Duplicated seat

PAX : Excuse me, Miss. There is someone in my seat.
F/A : May I see your boarding pass, please?

……

(to seated PAX) Excuse me, sir. May I see your boarding pass, please? I'm sorry, but I'm afraid there was a mistake in the seat arrangement. Would you please wait here for a moment while I check it for you?

……

Thank you for waiting, sir. Your seat has been rearranged.[1]
I'll guide you to your seat. Here is your seat. I'm very sorry for the inconvenience.

Alternative Expressions

1. The ground staff has assigned you a new seat.
   The ground staff has given you a new seat.

Dialogue 4_ Upgrade

PAX : Excuse me, Miss. I'd like to sit in the business class if there are any empty seats. Can I change my seat?
F/A : I'm very sorry, sir. We are not allowed to upgrade passenger seating during the flight.
PAX : Okay. I see.
F/A : Thank you for your understanding.

Dialogue 5_ Upgrade

PAX : Excuse me, Miss. May I get an upgrade to Business class?
F/A : Yes, sir. You can pay for your upgrade seat by credit card. Would you like me to find out the exact amount for you?
PAX : Yes, please.
F/A : Wait a moment, please.

Phrases Tips

다음 구문을 활용해 다양한 문장을 만들어 보세요.

All the seats are	occupied taken full	today.

I'm afraid there	has been a mistake was a mistake	in the seating arrangement. with the seating assignment.

Activity

다음 대화를 완성하세요.

<Separate seat>

PAX : Excuse me, Miss. My friend and I have been assigned separate seats. If ______________________________ , we would like to ________ together. Would it be possible?

F/A : ____

____

......

____

PAX : That's great. Where should ____?

F/A : Please take ____

____

PAX : Thank you very much.

F/A : ____

<Wrong seat>

PAX1 : ____

F/A : ____

(to PAX2) ____

____

Your seat is right behind this one.

PAX2 : Oh, I'm sorry.

PAX1 : That's OK.

F/A : (to PAX1) ________________________________

____

PAX1 : I'm fine. Thanks.

F/A : You're welcome.

<Duplicated seat>

PAX : Excuse me, Miss. There is someone in my seat.

F/A : ____

(to seated PAX) ________________________________

____

I'm sorry, but________________________________

Would you________________________________

......

Thank you for waiting, sir.

____

I'll guide you to your seat. Here is your seat. I'm very sorry for the inconvenience.

Reading Comprehension

다음을 읽고 물음에 답하세요.

Problems with Airline Seating Arrangement

The types of seat assignments on board may vary depending on the airline, but generally there are economy class, premium economy class, business class, and first class. Provided services may vary depending on the type of seat assignments, prices, and seat sizes.

As an example of airline seat assignments, some airlines provide services that allow passengers to select seats in advance without additional cost. Other airlines have adopted a method of assigning seats to passengers based on seat selection priority. In this case, passengers who have not selected seats in advance will be assigned seats from the remaining available seats.

In addition, some airlines may determine seat assignments based on passenger priority. For example, there are cases where seats are assigned to passengers with higher membership levels, disabilities, children, etc.

Complaints and problems arising from airline seat assignment errors are as follows.

Duplicate Reservation: If the same seat is reserved more than once, no other passenger will be able to select that seat.

Seat change: If a passenger's pre-selected seat is assigned to another passenger, the passenger will not be able to select the desired seat.

Family seat assignment: When family members or friends travel together, they may not be able to sit together.

Seat size: Passengers of certain airlines may find small size seats inconvenient.

Services: Passengers may not be able to receive the service they want because some airlines offer different services depending on their seating arrangements.

These problems can cause discontent among passengers, and airlines are improving their seating arrangement system to minimize these problems. Moreover, passengers can choose their seats in advance or contact the airline before boarding to be assigned the desired seats.

1. 좌석 배정 시 어떠한 서비스를 제공하나요?

____

____

2. 좌석 배정을 결정하는 승객 우선순위에는 어떤 것이 있나요?

____

____

3. 항공사가 좌석 배정을 잘못했을 때 생기는 불평과 문제는 무엇인가요?

____

____

UNIT 4

Ground Service

Words and Phrases

Match the words with the sentences.

bassinet　　vegetarian　　valuables　　pillow
garbage　　turbulence　　instead

1. Would you like The New York Times, ______________ ?
2. I want to confirm special meal that you requested.
   Did you request the ______________ meal?
3. Do you have any ______________ in your jacket/coat?
4. We will install a ______________ when the altitude stabilizes after take-off.
5. Can I have one more blanket and ______________ ?
6. I'll give you a plastic bag for ______________ .
7. Please hold your baby with your arms when the plane is shaken
   by ______________ .

Useful Expressions

1. Would you like to use headphones?
2. After everyone has boarded, I'll get it for you.
3. We've run out of that newspaper.
4. Here's the newspaper you asked for.
5. I'll check if we have any other newspaper.
6. I'm sorry, but I'm afraid the Chicago Tribune is not loaded on this flight.
7. I'll install a baby bassinet for your baby after take-off.
8. I'll get it for you in a moment.
9. Thank you for waiting.

Fadhli Adnan / Shutterstock.com

Conversation

Read the dialogues below and practice speaking with your partner by taking turns.

Dialogue 1_ Newspaper service

PAX : Excuse me, Miss. Do you have The Wall Street Journal?

F/A : Yes, sir. Just a moment, please. I'll get it for you right away.

......

Thank you for waiting, sir. Here's your newspaper.

PAX : Thanks.

F/A : You're welcome.

Dialogue 2_ Newspaper service

PAX : Excuse me, Miss. Can I have the Chicago Tribune?

F/A : I'm sorry, but I'm afraid the Chicago Tribune is not loaded on this flight. How about the Herald Tribune, instead?

PAX : That'll be fine.

F/A : Here you are, sir.

Dialogue 3_ Newspaper service

PAX : Do you have any other newspaper?

F/A : I'll check if we have any other newspaper, ma'am.

......

Thank you for waiting, ma'am. We have The New York Times and The Washington Post. Which one would you like?

PAX : I'll take The Washington Post.

F/A : Here you are, ma'am. Have a nice flight.

Dialogue 4_ Headphones service

F/A : Would you like to use headphones?
PAX : Yes, please.
F/A : Here are your headphones, sir.
PAX : Thanks.
F/A : No problem. Enjoy your flight.

Dialogue 5_ Headphones service

PAX : Excuse me, Miss. My headphones are not working properly. I can't hear anything.
F/A : Did you check to see if it's plugged in correctly?
PAX : Yes, I did.
F/A : Then it must be broken. I'm very sorry, ma'am. I'll bring you another one right away.
......
I'm sorry for making you waiting. Here are your new headphones. I'm sorry again for this inconvenience.

Dialogue 6_ Headphones service

F/A : Here are your headphones, ma'am.
PAX : Thank you, but I don't know how to use this audio system.
F/A : You can use the remote control or touch screen to select the main menu and your language. For more information on the A/V system, please refer to the entertainment magazine in your seat pocket.
PAX : Thank a lot.
F/A : It's my pleasure.

Dialogue 7_ Headphones service

F/A : Would you like to use headphones, sir?
PAX : Sure.
F/A : Here you are.
PAX : Thanks. What kind of music is available?
F/A : We have K-Pop, classical music, Japanese music, jazz and so on. You can get more information from the entertainment magazine in your seat pocket.
PAX : Thanks.
F/A : No problem, sir. Please enjoy your flight.

Dialogue 8_ Headphones service

F/A : Excuse me, ma'am. Here are your headphones.
PAX : Do I have to pay for this?
F/A : No, ma'am. It's free of charge.
PAX : Oh, really! Thank you.
F/A : My pleasure. Please enjoy your flight.

Dialogue 9_ Blanket service

PAX : Can I have one more blanket?
F/A : Sure, ma'am. I'll get it for you.
......
Thank you for waiting. Here's your blanket, ma'am.
PAX : Thanks.
F/A : My pleasure.

Dialogue 10_ Passenger with a baby

F/A : Good afternoon, ma'am. I am the duty crew in charge today. You can use this plastic bag for the garbage during the flight. If there is anything I can do for you, just let me know.

PAX : Thank you. Can I get a baby bassinet now?

F/A : Did you request a bassinet for your baby?

PAX : Yes, I did.

F/A : Then I'll install a bassinet after take-off. It is for you and your baby's safety, ma'am.

PAX : I see. Thank you.

(after take-off)

F/A : Excuse me, ma'am. Here is a baby bassinet. I'll set it up for you. But you have to hold your baby during turbulence for safety.

PAX : Yes. Thank you very much.

F/A : It's my pleasure, ma'am.

Dialogue 11_ Special meal

PAX : Excuse me, Miss. I'd like to know if my meal is loaded. I ordered a vegetarian meal.

F/A : Certainly, sir. May I have your name to check your special meal you've ordered?

PAX : My name is Matt Williams.

F/A : Thank you. Just a moment, please.

......

Sir, we have a vegetarian meal for you.

PAX : Oh, that's great. Thanks.

F/A : You're welcome.

In-flight Special Meals

✈ Child Meal (2~11 years old)

Child meals usually include menus such as spaghetti, fried rice, pizza, chicken, and more.

✈ Vegetarian Meal

Vegetarian diets mainly consist of grains, fruits, vegetables, and plant–based oils.

✈ Diabetic Meal

Diabetic meals are carefully prepared to balance the daily intake of calories, protein, fat, and sugar.

✈ Low-fat Meal

Provided only lean meat or fish without grease; high–cholesterol meat, egg yolks, and shellfish are avoided.

✈ Low-lactose Meal

Low lactose meal includes a meal without dairy products such as milk or cream.

✈ Kosher Meal

Kosher meal is prepared to comply with Jewish dietary requirements.

✈ Hindu Meal

A meal prepared without beef or veal based on Hindu traditions.

✈ Muslim Meal

Muslim meals are prepared in accordance with Halal method; do not include pork or alcohol.

Dialogue 12_ Flight time & Time lag

PAX : Excuse me, Miss. How long does it take to get New York today?
F/A : Our scheduled flight time after take-off will be 11 hours and 20 minutes, ma'am.
PAX : Thank you.
F/A : My pleasure.

Dialogue 13_ Flight time & Time lag

PAX : What time is it now in New York?
F/A : Seoul is 14 hours ahead of New York. So the local time in New York is 6:50 in the morning, sir.
PAX : Thanks.
F/A : My pleasure.

Dialogue 14_ Flight time & Time lag

PAX : Is there time lag between Seoul and Tokyo?
F/A : No, it isn't. There is no time difference between Seoul and Tokyo.
PAX : Thank you.
F/A : You are welcome.

The Ways to Tell Time

12 : 00 pm

noon

twelve pm

4 : 05 pm

four oh five in the afternoon

five past four

6 : 15 am

six fifteen in the morning

quarter past six

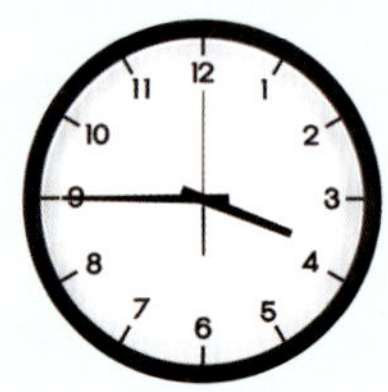

3 : 45 pm

three forty–five in the afternoon

quarter to four

10 : 30 pm

ten thirty at night

half past ten

8 : 50 am

eight fifty in the morning

ten to nine

12 : 00 am

midnight

twelve am

Dialogue 15_ Handling baggage in first/business class

F/A : Good morning, sir. Welcome aboard.
PAX : Good morning.
F/A : May I help you with your bags?
PAX : Yes, please.
F/A : Is there anything you might use during the flight?
PAX : I'll take my book and glasses.
F/A : Sure. I'll keep your bag in the coatroom and bring it back to you before landing. If there is anything you need during the flight, just let me know, sir.
PAX : Okay, thanks.
F/A : It's my pleasure.

Dialogue 16_ Handling coat in first/business class

F/A : Welcome aboard, sir. May I take your coat?
PAX : Yes, please.
F/A : Do you have any valuable items in your coat?
PAX : Yes, I do.
F/A : Then please keep them with you, sir.
PAX : Okay. I'll take my passport and purse out.
F/A : Thank you. I'll return it before landing.
PAX : Thank you.
F/A : You're welcome.

Phrases Tips

다음 구문을 활용해 다양한 문장을 만들어 보세요.

Would you like	to read a newspaper?
	to have bassinet for your baby ?
	a blanket and pillow?
	something to drink?

I will install a bassinet	after take-off for your baby's safety.
	once we are stable in the air after take-off.

I will get you	one new one another one	now.
		right away.

Activity

다음 문장을 이용하여 기내 대화를 만드세요.

1. I'm sorry, but I'm afraid the Chicago Tribune is not loaded on this flight.

   ____

2. Excuse me, Miss. My headphones are not working.

   ____

3. Do you have any other newspaper?

   ____

4. I'll get it for you in a moment.

   ____

5. Los Angeles is 16 hours behind Seoul.

   ____

6. Our scheduled flight time to Hong Kong is 3 hours and 10 minutes.

   ____

Reading Comprehension

다음을 읽고 물음에 답하세요.

In-flight Infant Passenger Service Management

Each airline may offer different infant services, but generally provides the following services:

1. Stroller rental: Strollers can be rented before and after boarding.
2. Infant meals: Provides meals for infants.
3. Infant bassinet: Provides infant seats with bassinet on board.
4. Diapers and wipes: Provides diapers and wipes on board if needed.
5. Infant toys: Provides infant toys.
6. Infant entertainment: Provides infant TV programs, movies, music, etc.
7. Priority boarding: Passengers traveling with infants have priority boarding.

Also, most airlines allow infants as young as 7 days old to board, but there is a growing number of passengers who complain about the crying of babies and cause dissatisfaction because of the noise. In one incident, passengers and parents argued over the crying of babies that echoed throughout the plane for four hours. Such occurrences may ruin the mood of passengers–sometimes provoke anger in extreme cases–who are trying to enjoy their trip. Therefore, some overseas airlines have introduced a no-kids zone. Flight attendants may apologize for excessive crying of babies, for instance, but it is difficult for them to intervene individually.

The following should be considered by the flight attendants for the child-and-parents passengers. First, it is crucial to provide a sense of stability to the parents when the child cries. Flight attendants can provide help by holding the child, for instance, to give the parents a chance to recoup, or by providing snacks or toys for the child. In addition, flight attendants can request understanding from other passengers and provide a quieter place, if available. Flight attendants should do their best to ensure that all passengers can travel comfortably.

1. 기내 유아 동반 승객에게 어떠한 서비스를 제공하나요?

____

____

____

2. 기내에서 어떤 승객 불만 사례가 발생했나요?

____

____

____

3. 승무원이 승객 불만을 최소화하기 위해 해야 하는 일은 무엇인가요?

____

____

____

UNIT 5

Preparation for Take-off

Words and Phrases

Match the words with the sentences.

fastened　　return　　upright　　flight mode

electronic devices　　lavatory　　window shade

1. You can not depart until all passengers have their seatbelts ______________ .

2. Please ______________ your seatback to the ______________ position.

3. All ______________ are prohibited during take-off and landing.

4. Is your cell phone set to ______________ ?

5. I'll let you know when you can use the ______________ safely.

6. Could you please open your ______________ ?

Useful Expressions

1. Please fasten your seatbelt.
2. Could you please bring your seatback to the upright position?
3. Would you please turn off your cell phone or put it on airplane mode?
4. Would you please close your tray table until after take-off?
5. We will be taking-off shortly.
6. would you please open your window shade?
7. Could you wait until after take-off?
8. Please place your carry-on bag underneath the seat in front of you until after take-off.
9. It's against airline regulation.
10. Would you mind holding your baby outside your seatbelt?
11. That will be more comfortable and safer for your baby.

Conversation

Read the dialogues below and practice speaking with your partner by taking turns.

Dialogue 1_ Seatbelt check

F/A : Excuse me, sir. Would you please fasten your seatbelt?
PAX : Yes.
F/A : Thank you.

Dialogue 2_ Seatbelt check

F/A : Hi, there. Could you fasten your seatbelt?
CHLD PAX : Do I have to?
F/A : Yes, you have to fasten your seatbelt for take-off.
CHLD PAX : Okay. But this belt is too big for me.
F/A : Let me put this pillow under your seatbelt.
How's that? Isn't that better?
CHLD PAX : Oh, much better. Thank you, ma'am.
F/A : No problem. Enjoy your flight.

Dialogue 3_ Baby's seatbelt

F/A : Excuse me, ma'am. Would you mind holding your baby outside your seatbelt?
PAX : Why?
F/A : It'll be more comfortable and safer for you and your baby.

Dialogue 4_ Seatback and tray table check

F/A : Excuse me, ma'am. Would you mind returning your seatback to the upright position?

PAX1 : Not at all.

F/A : Thank you. (to Pax2) Would you please close your tray table?

PAX2 : Sure. I will do that.

F/A : Thank you.

Dialogue 5_ Electronic devices check

F/A : Excuse me, sir. Would you please turn off your cell phone or put it on airplane mode? We will be taking-off very soon.

PAX : Can I just make one more phone call, please?

F/A : I'm very sorry, sir. But you have to turn it off right now. It's for your own safety.

PAX : Okay.

F/A : Thank you very much for your cooperation.

Dialogue 6_ Lavatory before take-off

F/A : Excuse me, sir. Could you please wait until take-off? We will be taking-off very shortly.

PAX : Okay.

F/A : Thank you for your cooperation. You can use the lavatory when the seatbelt sign is off.

Dialogue 7_ Baggage securing

F/A : Excuse me, ma'am. Would you please place your carry-on bag underneath the seat in front of you until after take-off.

PAX : Alright.

F/A : Thank you.

ANNOUNCEMENT Preparation for departure

Ladies and gentlemen, this is __________ Air flight _____________ bound for ____________ .

We are a few more minutes away from an on-time departure. Please make sure that your carry-on items are stored in the overhead bins or under the seat in front of you. Also, please take your assigned seat and fasten your seatbelt.

Thank you.

ANNOUNCEMENT Welcome

Good morning, ladies and gentlemen.

Captain Lee and all of our crew members are pleased to welcome you on board __________ Air, a __________ member.

This is flight ____________ bound for __________ .

Our flight time today will be _________ hour(s) and _________minute(s) after take-off.

During the flight, our cabin crew will be happy to serve you in any way we can.

Phrases Tips

다음 구문을 활용해 다양한 문장을 만들어 보세요.

We will be taking off	shortly. soon. in a minute.	We are about to (V)

Would you mind	opening your window shades, please?
	returning your tray table to the upright position, please?
	turning off your laptop for take-off, please?

Would you please	fasten your seatbelt?
	pull down the arm rest?
	close the tray table?
	hold your baby outside of your seatbelt?

Activity

다음 대화를 완성하세요.

F/A : Excuse me, sir. Would you please _________ your cell phone or ____________ it ____________ airplane mode? We will be taking-off very soon.

PAX : Can I just ____________ one more phone call, please?

F/A : I'm very sorry, sir. But you have to ____________ right now. It's for your own ____________ .

PAX : Okay.

F/A : Thank you very much for your ____________ .

다음 문장을 이용하여 기내 대화를 만드세요.

1. It's against airline regulation.

____

2. Would you mind holding your baby outside your seatbelt?

____

Reading Comprehension

다음을 읽고 물음에 답하세요.

Duties of Flight Attendants before take-off

Flight attendants, like passengers, place their personal belongings in places designated by the safety regulations. After storing their belongings, they change into room shoes (the shoes they wear only on the aircraft) and store other items in a compartment near the designated area. Then, they should check the service items, make sure that there are no issues with the in-flight safety and emergency equipment. Crews check everything from the most basic and important safety tasks to ensuring passengers have a safe and comfortable flight to their destination.

Each airline has its own manuals and checklists for cabin safety, and all crew members under the supervision of the cabin manager or supervisor will work in the designated areas. They also check whether in-flight broadcasts are clearly heard as well as the working status of personal monitors in the passenger seats. After the in-flight safety and security check, they return to the assigned work area to check the in-flight service items and rearrange them accordingly for easy use by the crew.

Due to the precautions and obligations of airplane emergency exit seat passengers, the emergency exit seat passengers are required to assist other passengers in emergency escape situations. The cabin crew must explain emergency escape assistance to passengers in emergency exit seats before take-off.

Only the passengers who meet the following conditions are allowed to sit in the emergency exit seats.

1. Passengers 15 years of age or older
2. Those who agree to and can implement emergency escape cooperation
3. Passengers who understand the instructions of the flight attendants and can verbally communicate to other passengers
4. Passengers who do not need help in case of an emergency escape
5. Passengers not required to assist accompanying passengers in the event of an emergency escape

1. 승무원이 기내 탑승 후 가장 먼저 하는 일은 무엇인가요?

____

____

2. 기내에서 점검해야 하는 것은 무엇인가요?

____

____

3. 비상구 좌석에 착석할 수 없는 승객은 어떤 사람인가요?

____

____

UNIT 6

Late Departure

Words and Phrases

Match the words with the sentences.

delayed connecting flight gate

technical problem working on due to

1. I'm going to miss my ______________ because of this delay.
2. I'm sorry, but this flight has been ______________ .
3. Why are we sill at the __________ ?
4. There is a __________________ with the plane.
5. The mechanics are now _________________ it.
6. There is a delay _____________ the bad weather.

Useful Expressions

1. We are waiting for some passengers to come on board.
2. We are waiting for the departure documents to arrive.
3. Our take-off has been delayed because we have many airplanes in front of us that are waiting to take-off.
4. It's due to traffic congestion at the airport.
5. We expected to depart in 15 minutes.
6. We're waiting for the departure clearance from the control tower.
7. We're waiting for the baggage to be loaded.
8. We will be taking-off as soon as they arrive.
9. I'm sorry for the inconvenience.

Conversation

Read the dialogues below and practice speaking with your partner by taking turns.

Dialogue 1_ Reason for delay

PAX : Why aren't we leaving yet?

F/A : I'm very sorry, but we will be delayed for a while.

PAX : Why?

F/A : We're waiting for some connecting passengers to come on board. We'll be taking-off as soon as they arrive. I'm sorry for the inconvenience.

Dialogue 2_ Reason for delay

PAX : Excuse me, Miss. Why are we still on the ground?

F/A : I'm sorry ma'am. We are waiting the departure clearance from the control tower. We're expecting to take-off in 5 minutes.

PAX : Okay. I see.

Dialogue 3_ Reason for delay

PAX : Why aren't we moving yet?

F/A : We are waiting for some departure documents. We will be taking-off soon. I'm sorry for the inconvenience, ma'am.

Dialogue 4_ Reason for delay

PAX : Excuse me, Miss. What's the reason for the delay?

F/A : I'm very sorry, but it's due to congestion at the airport. There are a few more airplanes in front of us that are waiting to take-off.

PAX : Then when will we depart?

F/A : We expect to depart in 10 minutes. I'm sorry for the inconvenience.

ANNOUNCEMENT Seatbelt sign off

Ladies and gentlemen, the captain has turned off the seatbelt sign.

In case of any unexpected turbulence, we strongly recommend you keep your seatbelt fastened at all times while seated.

Please use caution when opening the overhead bins as the contents may fall out.

For more information about service available on this flight, please refer to the ○○○○ magazine in your seat pocket.

Phrases Tips

다음 구문을 활용해 다양한 문장을 만들어 보세요.

Be supposed to + V ~해야 한다 ~하기로 되어 있다	You are supposed to fasten your seatbelt.
	You are supposed to start boarding in 15 minutes.
	You are supposed to depart/leave at 4:00 pm.

This flight	will be delayed.
	has been canceled.
	has been delayed.

Activity

다음 대화를 완성하세요.

PAX : Excuse me. Why are we still on the ground?

F/A : I'm very sorry, but we're waiting ____________ to come on ______________ . We will _______________ as _______________ they _______________ . I'm sorry for _______________ .

PAX : Excuse me. It's 5:20. We were supposed to depart at 5:00. What's ____________ the delay?

F/A : I'm terribly sorry, but our flight __________________ . The audio system of this plane has a minor problem, so the ___________ are trying to _________ it now.

PAX : Oh my god!!! I might Miss my ________________________ due to this delay!!!

F/A : I'm so sorry, sir. We will try to fix the problem and take-off as quickly as possible.

다음 상황을 이용하여 대화를 연습해 보세요.

1. 기체의 작은 결함으로 인한 이륙 지연
2. 연결편 승객으로 인한 이륙 지연
3. 공항 혼잡으로 인한 이륙 지연

Reading Comprehension

다음을 읽고 물음에 답하세요.

Cause of Airline Departure Delay

There are various reasons and causes for flight delays. Among them, the most common cause is weather conditions. For safety reasons, aircraft can postpone or cancel take-off when weather conditions such as fog, heavy rain, snow, and strong winds are not favorable.

In addition, take-off can also be delayed if inspection or repair is required before departure. Also, there may be problems within the airport that cause flight delays. For example, if passengers or luggage are Missing or misplaced before the aircraft departs, the departure may be delayed. Additionally, departure may be delayed due to problems with the airport's internal systems or a shortage of personnel.

Furthermore, there are also problems that occur at airports with high air traffic volume. Since there is a risk of collision with other aircrafts during take-off or landing, airports operate a system to control the take-off and landing of aircrafts. However, if this system does not work smoothly or if the aircraft's operating plan changes, certain departures may be delayed.

Finally, there are also passenger-related issues that can cause flight delays. If passengers are delayed boarding or if problems occur after boarding, the departure may be delayed. For example, if a passenger refuses to board or if a passenger blocks the emergency exit, the departure may be delayed. Therefore, understanding and complying with aircraft operations are necessary.

Especially during the vacation season, cases of consumer losses due to flight delays or cancellations are increasing and, as standards vary by countries, many airlines show lukewarm attitudes, making it difficult for consumers to receive proper compensation. Generally, for domestic flights, compensation of up to 10% is paid for delays of more than 1 hour, and for international flights, compensation of up to 10% is paid for delays of 2 to 4 hours, and most airlines provide compensation. However, compensation is based on the time of arrival at the final destination, not the departure time.

1. 비행기 지연을 일으키는 가장 흔한 원인은 무엇인가요?

   ____

   ____

2. 항공기 및 인력으로 인한 지연에는 어떤 내용이 있나요?

   ____

   ____

3. 항공기 출발 지연 시 어떠한 보상을 받을 수 있나요?

   ____

   ____

PART

2

In-flight Service

UNIT 7

Towel & Beverage Service

Words and Phrases

Match the words with the sentences.

compensate　　on the rocks　　chaser　　something

wipe　　take　　be made of

1. It ________________ Jin and tonic water.
2. Would you like ____________ to drink, sir ?
3. Here is your scotch. Would you care for a ____________ ?
4. Are you finished with your drink? May I ____________ your cup?
5. I'll get you something to ________________ right away.
6. How would you like your whisky, straight or ____________ ?
7. Here is a cleaning coupon. Just take it to the airlines office, and then the airlines will ____________ you. Once again, I'm sorry.

Useful Expressions

1. Would you like(care for) something to drink?
2. Would you like(care for) a glass of wine?
3. Would you like(care for) some more drink?
4. Would you like(care for) some juice?
5. Would you please open your tray table?
6. We only have orange, pineapple, and tomato juice.
7. How would you like your coffee(vodka, whisky, etc)?
8. Would you like another beer?
9. Could you tell me how it's made?
10. What kind of juice would you like?
11. Would you like some ice in your drink?
12. Which one would you like?
13. Would you like to have your whisky, straight or on the rocks?
14. I'm sorry, but I'm afraid we don't serve vegetable juice.
15. Please enjoy your drink.
16. Excuse me, the cart is passing by.
17. Would you like some chaser?
18. May I take away your glass?
19. May I take your cup if you're finished?
20. May I take this away?

Conversation

Read the dialogues below and practice speaking with your partner by taking turns.

Dialogue 1_ Towel service

F/A : Would you like a hot towel?[1]

PAX : Yes, please.

F/A : Here's your towel. Please be careful. It's very hot.

......

Are you finished with your towel?[2]

Alternative Expressions

1. Would you care for a hot towel?
2. Have you finished with your towel?
   May I take your towel?
   Would you please put it in the basket?
   May I have your towel?
   Could you put the towel in the basket?

Dialogue 2_ Drink service

F/A : Excuse me, sir. Would you like something to drink before dinner?

PAX : Yes, please. What kind of drinks do you have?

F/A : We offer a variety of beverages including soft drinks, juices, whisky, and beer. What would you like?

PAX : I'll have a coke.

F/A : Certainly, sir. Would you like some ice in it?

PAX : Yes, please.

F/A : Here's your coke, sir.

PAX : Thanks.

Dialogue 3_ Drink service

F/A : Excuse me, ma'am. Would you care for something to drink before your meal? We have juices, soft drinks, beer, whisky, and vodka.

PAX : What kind of juice do you have?

F/A : We have orange, pineapple, tomato and guava juice. Which one would you like?

PAX : May I have a glass of guava juice?

F/A : Certainly, ma'am. Just a moment, please. Here's your guava juice.

PAX : Thank you.

F/A : Enjoy your drink.

Dialogue 4_ Drink service

F/A : Excuse me, ma'am. Would you care for something to drink before your meal?

PAX : Yes, can I have an apple juice, please?

F/A : I'm sorry, ma'am. We don't have an apple juice on board. Would you like some pineapple juice, instead?

PAX : Alright. I'll have it.

F/A : Thank you, ma'am. Here's your juice.

PAX : Thanks.

F/A : You're welcome, ma'am.

Dialogue 5_ Whisky service

F/A : Good evening, sir. Would you like something to drink?

PAX : Sure. Do you have vodka?

F/A : Yes, sir. How would you like your vodka?

PAX : Could you make a glass of Blood Mary?

F/A : Certainly, sir. One moment, please.

......

Here's your drink.

PAX : Thanks a lot.

F/A : It's my pleasure. Enjoy your drink.

Dialogue 6_ Whisky service

F/A : Excuse me, sir. Can I get you something to drink?
PAX : Yes, can I have a whisky, please?
F/A : Sure, sir. How would you like your whisky?
PAX : On the rocks, please.
F/A : Certainly, sir. Here's your whisky on the rocks.
PAX : Thanks.
F/A : You're welcome.

Dialogue 7_ Cocktail service

F/A : Excuse me, ma'am. Would you care for something to drink?
PAX : Can I have a gin and tonic?
F/A : Certainly, ma'am. One moment, please.
......
Here's your drink, ma'am.
PAX : Thanks.
......
F/A : How's your drink?
PAX : Actually, it is a little strong(weak). Would you add some more tonic water(gin)?
F/A : Sure, ma'am.
......
How is it?
PAX : Very good.
F/A : Please enjoy your drink.

Dialogue 8_ Cocktail service

F/A : Excuse me, sir. Would you care for something to drink?
PAX : Yes, I'd like to have a Blue Hawaii.
F/A : I'm sorry, but I'm afraid I don't know how it's made.
PAX : It's made of rum and pineapple juice.
F/A : I'm very sorry, sir. But we don't have rum on board. Would you like something else, instead?
PAX : What would you recommend?
F/A : I'd like to recommend a Chi Chi. It's made of vodka and pineapple juice.
PAX : Alright. I'll try it.
......
F/A : Here's your drink, sir. Would you like some nuts with your drink?
PAX : Oh! yes, please.
F/A : Here you are. I hope you enjoy this one.

Dialogue 9_ Beer service

PAX : Excuse me, Miss. Can I have one more beer?
F/A : Sure, sir. Just a moment, please.
......
Here's your beer.

Dialogue 10_ Cocktail service

PAX : Excuse, me. Could I have another drink?
F/A : Certainly, sir. You were drinking scotch and water, weren't you?
PAX : Yes, you're right.
F/A : Just a moment, sir. I'll bring you your drinks soon.
......
Here you are. I'll take your empty glass. Please enjoy your drink.

Dialogue 11_ Cup collecting

F/A : Excuse me, ma'am. Are you finished with your drink?
PAX : Yes, I am.
F/A : I'll take your cup. Thank you.

Dialogue 12_ Cup collecting

F/A : Excuse me, ma'am. Are you finished with your drink?
PAX : I'm not quite finished yet.

<case 1>
F/A : I'm sorry, ma'am. Take your time.

<case 2>
F/A : I'm sorry, ma'am. Would you care for a fresh drink?
PAX : Oh! That would be nice.
F/A : Just a moment, please.
......
Here's a new one.

Dialogue 13_ Cup collecting

F/A : Excuse me, ma'am. (Did you enjoy your drink?) May I take your cup?
PAX : Yes, please.
F/A : Thank you.

Dialogue 14_ Spilled drink

F/A : I am terribly sorry, ma'am. Let me get something to clean it up with.[1]

……

Ma'am, may I help you clean it up?

PAX : That's all right. Never mind.

F/A : I am really sorry, ma'am. I'll bring you another drink right away.

……

Here's your drink.

Alternative Expressions

1. I'll get something to wipe that off for you.

Dialogue 15_ Spilled drink

〈얼룩의 정도가 심한 경우〉

F/A : Excuse me, ma'am. Here's a cleaning coupon. You can take it to any Star Air office and they will reimburse you. I'm sorry again, ma'am.

Phrases Tips

다음 구문을 활용해 다양한 문장을 만들어 보세요.

something to + V(동사) ~할 것	
	something to drink
	something to read
	something to eat
	something to watch

something + A(형용사) ~한 것	
	something warm
	something cold
	something chilled
	something soft

Are you	finished done	with your towel? with your drink? with your meal?

Activity

다음 대화를 완성하세요.

F/A : Excuse me, sir. Can I ______________________ to drink?

PAX : Yes, Can I have a whisky, please?

F/A : Sure, sir. How ____ ?

PAX : On the rocks, please.

F/A : Certainly, sir. Here's your whisky on the rocks.

PAX : Thanks.

F/A : You're welcome.

F/A : Excuse me, ma'am. Would ____ drink before your meal?

PAX : Yes, Can I have an apple juice, please?

F/A : I'm sorry, ma'am. We ____________________________________ on board. Would you like some pineapple juice, _________ ?

PAX : Alright. I'll have it.

F/A : Thank you, ma'am. Here's your juice.

PAX : Thanks.

F/A : You're welcome, ma'am.

F/A : Excuse me, sir. Would you __________ something to drink?

PAX : Yes, I'd _____________ a Blue Hawaii.

F/A : I'm sorry, but __________________________________

PAX : It's __________________________________ rum and pineapple juice.

F/A : I'm very sorry, sir. But we don't have rum on board. ____________________

_______________ ?

PAX : What would you recommend?

F/A : I'd like to recommend a Chi Chi. It's ___________ vodka and pineapple juice.

PAX : Alright. I'll try it.

....

F/A : Here's your drink, sir. ______________________ nuts ______ your drink?

PAX : Oh! Yes, please.

F/A : Here you are. I hope you enjoy this one.

F/A : I am terribly sorry, ma'am. ____

(____)

....

Ma'am, may I ____ ?

PAX : That's all right. Never mind.

F/A : I am really sorry, ma'am. I'll ____________________________ right away.

....

Here's your drink.

〈얼룩의 정도가 심한 경우〉

F/A : Excuse me, ma'am. Here's ______________ You ______________________

____ I'm sorry again, ma'am.

Reading Comprehension

다음을 읽고 물음에 답하세요.

Accidents that Occur During In-flight Beverage Service

When serving drinks on board, flight attendants should prioritize passenger safety. When providing drinks, they should encourage passengers to receive drinks cautiously, especially hot drinks.

Injury caused by beverage cart

Mark suffered a serious injury when his knee collided with the beverage service cart while sitting in a seat near the aisle of the airplane. While it is rare for the service cart to brush against a shoulder, foot, or arm as it passes by, it is common for elbows, feet, or knees to be severely injured. Passengers must be made aware that the cart is passing by and take extreme caution when it is moving to prevent accidents.

Child burned by tilted coffee pot

The flight attendants of U Airlines Flight 430 were serving drinks and snacks to passengers from the beverage cart parked in the aisle. Suddenly, the coffee pot fell off the cart and onto a child nearby. The child was in so much pain that the doctor on board rushed to treat the child. The flight attendants declared a medical emergency and had to divert the plane to the nearest airport to treat the child's burn injuries. The investigation revealed that the improper placement of the coffee pot and the failure to use a safe lid were the cause of the child's injury.

What to do after getting burned on a plane?

Immediately immerse the affected area in cold water. Cold water cools the burned area, reduces pain, and disinfects the area. If it is difficult to immerse the burned area in water, rinse it gently with clean water. Be careful not to rub or touch the burned area.

If the burned area is extensive, emergency treatment may be necessary to help the patient avoid shock. If there is a doctor on the plane, medical professionals can treat wounds and prevent infection with proper treatment. This can be more difficult in enclosed environments such as the cabin but flight attendants should do everything they can to help.

1. 음료를 서비스할 때 가장 우선시되는 것은 무엇인가요?

____

____

2. 마크는 비행기 안에서 어떠한 일을 겪었나요?

____

____

3. 화상을 입은 경우 어떠한 조치가 필요한가요?

____

____

UNIT 8

Meal Service

Words and Phrases

Match the words with the sentences.

run out of   as well   a glass of   a variety of

mixed vegetables   decaffeinated   appetizer

1. I'm sorry, but we have ________________ Korean meal.
2. Can I get you something to drink ______________ ?
3. It is a Korean traditional rice meal with ______________ vegetables.
4. We will have potato wedges for an _______________ .
5. Can I have _________________ red wine, please?
6. The chicken is a meal with fried noodles and __________________ .
7. Do you have ________________ coffee?

Useful Expression

1. We will be serving dinner soon.
2. Would you like to have breakfast?
3. Would you please open your tray table?
4. May I set up your tray table now?
5. Would you please return your seatback for the passenger behind you?
6. We have beef and fish with broccoli. Which one would you prefer?
7. What would you like, Bibimbap or fish?
8. We've run out of the beef. How about fish, instead?
9. We are heating up your meal now. It'll be ready in a few minutes.
10. Would you like something to drink with your meal?
11. Have you ever tried Bibimbap before?
12. Bibimbap is a Korean traditional dish. It contains rice, vegetables, minced beef, sesame oil, and Korean spicy paste.
13. Here's your seaweed soup. It's very hot. Please be careful.
14. This is Korean style dipping sauce.
15. Would you care for some(more) wine? We have red wine and white wine.
16. I hope you enjoy your meal.
17. Would you like some tea/coffee/cream and sugar? We have green tea and black tea.
18. Would you please put your cup on this tray?
19. Would you like some lemon with your tea?
20. Another cabin crew will serve coffee soon.
21. Can I get you anything else?
22. Did you enjoy your meal? May I take your tray?

Conversation

Read the dialogues below and practice speaking with your partner by taking turns.

Dialogue 1_ Meal service

F/A : Excuse me, sir. We have beef with chilly bean sauce and fish. Which one would you prefer?

PAX : I will take the beef, please.

F/A : No problem. Can I get you something to drink as well?

PAX : Yes, I'd like some red wine, please.

F/A : Certainly, sir. I hope you enjoy your meal.

Dialogue 2_ Meal service

F/A : Excuse me, ma'am. We're serving dinner now. Would you please open your tray table?

PAX : Sure.

F/A : Thank you. Today, we have Bibimbap and chicken with fried rice. Which one would you like?

PAX : Can I have a Bibimbap?

F/A : Certainly, ma'am. Here you are.

PAX : Thank you.

F/A : Please enjoy your meal.

Dialogue 3_ Meal service–allergic to seafood

F/A : Excuse me, sir. We are serving lunch now.

PAX : What's the meal today?

F/A : We have fish with steamed rice.

PAX : Ah, I'm sorry, but I am allergic to seafood. Do you have anything else?

F/A : I'm sorry, but we only serve fish on this portion. But I'll check if we have anything else to serve you. Just a moment, please.

PAX : Thanks.

F/A : My pleasure.

......

We only have some bread and salad. Would you like some bread and salad for your lunch?

PAX : That would be great. Thanks a lot.

F/A : Here you are. If there is anything I can get for you, just let me know.

Dialogue 4_ Meal service

F/A : Excuse me, ma'am. What would you like to have for your dinner? We have a choice of Bibimbap and beef with brocoli.

PAX : What's Bibimbap?

F/A : Bibimbap is a Korean traditional dish. It contains rice, vegetables, minced beef, sesame oil, and Korean spicy paste.

PAX : It sounds good. I'll try the Bibimbap. Could you tell me how to eat it?

F/A : Certainly, sir. It is easy. Just put the rice, sesame oil and hot pepper paste into the bowl, then mix them together. If you don't like spicy food, you can eat without hot paste.

PAX : Oh, don't worry. I love spicy food.

F/A : I hope you enjoy your meal, ma'am.

Dialogue 5_ Meal service–run out

PAX : Excuse me. I'd like to have the fish.

F/A : I'm very sorry, sir, but I'm afraid we've run out of the fish.[1]
We only have beef available.[2] Is that be alright, sir?

PAX : Alright. I'll take the beef.

F/A : Here you are. Would you like some wine with your beef?

Alternative Expressions

1. We are all out of the fish. We don't have the fish any more.
2. We only have beef left.

Dialogue 6_ Meal service–served later

F/A : Excuse me, ma'am. We have beef and chicken. Which one would you prefer?

PAX : I am not really hungry now. Can I have my meal later?

F/A : Certainly, sir. Please let us know when you would like to eat your meal.[1]

PAX : Thanks.

F/A : You're welcome.

Alternative Expressions

1. Please let me know when you want to be served.

Dialogue 7_ Meal service–before landing

F/A : Excuse me, ma'am. We have beef and fish today. Which one would you prefer?

PAX : Actually, I'm not really hungry right now. Can I have my meal a little later?

F/A : I'm very sorry, sir. But we will be landing in about an hour. So we won't have enough time to serve your meal.

PAX : That's okay.

F/A : Would you like something to drink?

PAX : No thanks.

F/A : If you need anything else, just let us know.

Dialogue 8_ Special meal service

F/A : Excuse me, sir. Are you Linda Brezinsky?

PAX : Yes, I am.

F/A : Did you request a vegetarian meal?

PAX : Yes, I did.

F/A : Here's your meal, ma'am. Please enjoy your meal.

Dialogue 9_ Special meal service

F/A : Excuse me, sir. Did you request a kosher meal?

PAX : Yes, I did.

F/A : This is the kosher meal you requested.
Would you like to open it yourself?

PAX : Yes, I'd like to.

F/A : Thank you. May I heat it up for you?

PAX : Yes, please.

......

F/A : Thank you for waiting, sir.
Here you are. I hope you enjoy your meal.

Dialogue 10_ Special meal service

PAX : Excuse me, Miss. When I made my reservation, I requested a diabetic meal.

F/A : I am sorry, ma'am. May I have your name, please?

PAX : My name is James Clooney.

F/A : I'll check it for you right away.

<case 1>

F/A : I'm sorry for waiting. We're heating up your meal now. It will be ready in a few minutes.

......

Here's your meal, ma'am. Is there anything I can get for you?

PAX : Thanks. Can I have some diet-coke?

F/A : Certainly, sir.

<case 2>

F/A : I'm terribly sorry, ma'am. There was a mistake and your diabetic meal wasn't loaded in Seoul. Would you mind telling me what would you like? I'll try my best to prepare it.

PAX : Then can I just have some salad without dressing?

F/A : Sure, sir. I'll bring some salad right away.

......

Here's your salad, ma'am. I'm sorry, again. If there's anything you need, just let me know.

Dialogue 11_ Special meal service–without reservation

PAX : Excuse me, Miss. Can I have a vegetarian meal?

F/A : Did you request a vegetarian meal when you made your reservation?

PAX : No, I didn't.

F/A : I'm sorry, sir, but you should order your special meal in advance. We don't have any vegetarian meal on board, but I can serve you some salad. Would that be okay for you?

PAX : That would be great. Thank you.

F/A : No problem.

Dialogue 12_ Special meal service

PAX : Excuse me, Miss. I don't think my meal is hot enough.

F/A : Oh, I'm very sorry, sir. I'll heat it up for you right away.

......

Thank you for waiting. Here's your meal. I'm sorry for this inconvenience.

Dialogue 13_ Hot beverage service

F/A : Would you like some coffee?

PAX : Yes, please.

F/A : Would you please put your cup on the tray?

......

Thank you. Here's your coffee, ma'am. Please be careful. It's very hot. Would you like some cream and sugar with your coffee?

PAX : No thanks.

F/A : Please enjoy your coffee.

Dialogue 14_ Hot beverage service

F/A : Would you like some coffee, sir?

PAX : I'd like to drink coffee, but I'm afraid I can't sleep well.

F/A : Then how about decaffeinated coffee? We have Sanka.

PAX : It sounds great. Let me have it.

F/A : Please wait a moment. I'll get it for you right away.

......

Thank you for waiting, sir. Here's your decaffeinated coffee.

PAX : Thanks a lot.

F/A : It's my pleasure, sir.

Dialogue 15_ Hot beverage service

F/A1 : Would you care for some coffee?

PAX : Do you have tea?

F/A1 : Yes, we do. Another cabin crew will serve you tea soon.

PAX : Oh, I see.

......

F/A2 : Would you like some tea?

PAX : Yes, please.

F/A2 : May I have your cup, please?

......

Here's your tea, ma'am. Please be careful. It's very hot. Would you like some lemon with your tea?

PAX : Yes, please.

F/A2 : Here's your lemon. Enjoy your tea, ma'am.

Dialogue 16_ Meal tray collecting

F/A : Excuse me, ma'am. Did you enjoy your meal?
PAX : Yes. I loved it.
F/A : Thanks. May I take your meal tray?[1]
PAX : Yes, please.
F/A : Thank you.

Alternative Expressions

1. May I clear off your meal tray?

Dialogue 17_ Meal tray collecting

F/A : Excuse me, ma'am. Are you finished with your meal?
PAX : Yes, I am.
F/A : Thanks. May I take this away?
PAX : Yes, please.
F/A : Thank you.

Phrases Tips

다음 구문을 활용해 다양한 문장을 만들어 보세요.

run out of ~를 다 써버리다	run out of money
	run out of the white wine
	run out of the chicken

use up ~를 써버리다	use up the toilet paper
	use up my energy
	use up my pocket money

May I have your Please put your Would you please place your	cup	please on my tray

What? (×)
Excuse me? (○) I beg your pardon? (○) Come again? (○) Pardon me? (○)

Activity

다음 질문에 답하세요.

1. Today's menu is beef and fish. Your passenger loves beef, but unfortunately, all the beef have been served. What are you going to do for your passenger?

____

____

____

____

____

2. One of your passengers asks for his vegetarian meal. However the meal is not loaded. What can you do?

____

____

____

____

____

다음 기내 대화를 완성하세요.

F/A : Excuse me, sir. We are ________ lunch now.

PAX : What's the meal today?

F/A : We have fish with steamed rice.

PAX : Ah, I'm sorry, but I am allergic to seafood. Do you have anything else?

F/A : I'm sorry, ____

____

Just a moment, please.

PAX : Thanks.

F/A : My pleasure.

....

____

____?

PAX : That would be great. Thanks a lot.

F/A : Here you are. If ______________________________ I can get for you, just let me know.

F/A : Excuse me, ma'am. What ___________________________for your dinner?

We have __________ of Bibimbap and beef with brocoli.

PAX : What's Bibimbap?

F/A : Bibimbap is ____

It ____

____________________ and Korean spicy paste.

PAX : It sounds good. I'll try the Bibimbap. ______________________________ it?

F/A : Certainly, sir. It is easy.

Just put ____

____

____

If ____________________________, you can eat it ______ hot paste.

PAX : Oh, don't worry. I love spicy food.

F/A : I hope you enjoy your meal, ma'am.

F/A : Excuse me, ma'am. We have beef and fish today.

____?

PAX : Actually, I'm not really hungry right now.

____ later?

F/A : I'm very sorry, sir.

____

____

PAX : That's okay.

F/A : Would ______________________________?

PAX : No thanks.

F/A : If ______________________________ know.

PAX : Excuse me, Miss. When I made my reservation, I requested a diabetic meal.

F/A : I'm sorry, ma'am. ______________________________?

PAX : My name is James Clooney.

F/A : I'll check it for you right away.

<case 1>

F/A : Thank you for waiting. We're ________________________________

It will ____

......

Here's your meal, ma'am. Is there anything I can get for you?

PAX : Thanks. Can I have some diet-coke?

F/A : Certainly, sir.

<case 2>

F/A : I'm terribly sorry, ma'am. ________________________________

Would ____ like?

I'll try ____ it.

PAX : Then can I just have some salad without dressing?

F/A : Sure, sir. I'll ______________________________away.

......

Here's your salad, ma'am. I'm sorry, again.

If ____ know.

Reading Comprehension

다음을 읽고 물음에 답하세요.

Complaints from Passengers During In-flight Meal Services

1. Cases where the taste is bad or the selection is limited
2. Cases where the meal is delayed or the serving is late
3. Cases where the food is not warm or fresh enough
4. Cases where the meal portion is too small
5. Cases where the meal causes an allergic reaction

Recently, there was a case of dissatisfaction with in-flight meal service where a passenger was returning from a honeymoon trip to Hawaii and departing for Incheon from the Honolulu Airport. While eating the in-flight meal, foreign matter came out from the food and caused injury. A glass fragment was found in the bibimbap, and three teeth were damaged. The passenger said that while taking a picture of the bibimbap before eating, he spat out a glass fragment with a cracking sound. After that, he went to the hospital and received a diagnosis of two vertical fractures and one enamel fracture. The airline offered 5,000 miles compensation, but after receiving the hospital diagnosis, they offered 20,000 miles compensation. The airline is conducting its own investigation and has announced that it will fully compensate for immediate dental treatment.

In addition, some passengers of recent airlines have shared their disappointment with the meals provided in economy class, along with photos, and raised complaints that the quality of in-flight meals has declined. A passenger who boarded B Airlines in the United States was angry that the only option was a vegetarian meal, and the airline crew's response was rude, making him even more angry. He asked to speak to the captain and, when his request was not accepted, he stood up and started to complain. He did not actually try to access the cockpit, but he did not follow the instructions to sit down and started pushing the crew and causing a disturbance.

He was restrained with the help of other passengers and was arrested by the airport police at the destination on charges of assaulting a crew member and obstructing business. The airline is implementing education programs that can help prevent certain situations as well as addressing issues in advance and is making efforts to resolve the problem.

1. 기내식 서비스에서 발생하는 불평 5가지는 무엇인가요?

____

____

2. 첫 번째 기내식 불만 사례 내용과 보상 방법은 무엇인가요?

____

____

3. 두 번째 기내식 불만 사례 내용과 해결 방법은 무엇인가요?

____

____

UNIT 9

In-flight Entertainment

Words and Phrases

Match the words with the sentences.

select　out of order　volume　unplug
operate　control panel　be attached to

1. Please show me how to ________________ the movie I want to watch.
2. I'm afraid that the sound of this seat is ________________ .
3. You can control the ________________ by pressing these buttons.
4. You should ________________ earphones first to put this headphones.
5. This magazine show you how to ________________ this control panel.
6. Please use the ________________ to change or select the movies.
7. The control panel ________________ your armrest on your right side.

Useful Expressions

1. This magazine has more details about in-flight entertainment.
2. May I check it for you?
3. The movies are listed in the in-flight magazine.
4. It seems that there is a problem with the screen.
5. It seems that the sound system is out of order.
6. The sound system in this seat is out of order.
7. Would you like to move to this seat, ma'am?
8. I'll check if we have any empty seats.
9. I'll check and let you know.
10. I'm sorry for the inconvenience.
11. Would you please close your window shade?
12. You can recharge your phone in your seat.
13. We have an in-seat-power-supply underneath your seat for recharging.

Conversation

Read the dialogues below and practice speaking with your partner by taking turns.

Dialogue 1_ Window shade

F/A : Excuse me, sir. Would you please close your window shade? It's hard to see the screen with the window shade open, ma'am.
PAX : Oh, I see.
F/A : Thank you.
PAX : No problem.

Dialogue 2_ Extra earphones

PAX : Excuse me, Miss. Can I have another earphones? I don't think they are working.
F/A : I'm really sorry, ma'am. I'll bring new earphones right away.
......
Here you are. Would you please try them? Are they working?
PAX : No, I can hear nothing.
F/A : I'm very sorry, but I'm afraid the sound system in this seat is out of order. Let me check if we have any empty seat.
......
Thank you for waiting, ma'am. We have some empty seats in the front of the cabin. Would you like to move to that seat?
PAX : Okay.
F/A : Please follow me, and I'll guide you. I'm really sorry for the inconvenience. I hope you will enjoy the movie.

Dialogue 3_ Operate panel

PAX : Excuse me, Miss. I'd like to watch a movie. Would you please tell what I have to do with this panel?

F/A : Sure, ma'am. Did you plug in your headphones?

PAX : Yes.

F/A : Okay. Then press this button to select a movie, or you just can touch the screen here. And you can turn up or down the volume by pressing these two buttons.

PAX : Oh, that's simple.

F/A : Yes, it's not that difficult. Also you can refer to the magazine in your seat pocket. It shows you how to operate the control panel.

PAX : Thank you very much.

F/A : It's my pleasure. Enjoy your movie, ma'am.

Phrases Tips

다음 구문을 활용해 다양한 문장을 만들어 보세요.

Let's move to	the other seat another seat
Shall we move to	
Why don't you move to	
How about moving to	
What about moving to	

Let me	take a look. have a look.
I will just	
Allow me to	

Activity

다음 문장을 이용하여 기내 대화를 만드세요.

1. Hello, Miss. I don't know how to control this handset. Can you help me?

2. Excuse me, my headphone doesn't work.

Reading Comprehension

다음을 읽고 물음에 답하세요.

Development and Growth of In-flight Entertainment

As the name suggests, in-flight entertainment refers to the concept of services available on board such as games, movies, music, and entertainment that can be enjoyed during the flight. With the advancement of electronics engineering, in-flight entertainment has also evolved and transformed over time. In the early days after the birth of airplanes, electronic devices were not as developed, and in-flight entertainment was limited to magazines and newspapers.

As LCD technology became more popular and affordable, airlines started installing individual monitors, or Personal TVs, in each seat to differentiate themselves from other airlines. With the development of touchscreen technology, the on-demand audio and video (AVOD) systems were finally introduced. Passengers could now select and operate their desired videos, music, and flight information, expanding the range of choices compared to the previous Personal TV (PTV) era.

Major domestic airlines continuously update their in-flight AVOD systems with over 300 movies and the latest popular K-contents to provide passengers an enjoyable and impressive air travel experience. Additionally, they have introduced in-flight Wi-Fi services, starting with international routes, and plan to expand the service to all domestic routes gradually on various aircraft models.

KIM, who works for a large company, used the in-flight Wi-Fi service on a business trip to New York. There were many situations where they needed to stay in constant contact with colleagues or superiors and carry out work tasks, so they decided to use the in-flight Wi-Fi. The aircraft model (A350) had Wi-Fi available, and after paying around 30,000 won for unlimited usage, they were highly satisfied with the experience. Although the internet was slow and there were frequent disconnections, it didn't pose a major obstacle for exchanging messages or conducting internet searches. The ability to handle work tasks during the flight alone was impressive, and they anticipate using it on future business trips. They also believe that in addition to business trips, they will find it convenient to use in-flight Wi-Fi for planning itineraries or making changes to accommodations while traveling.

1. 전자기술이 발전하기 전에는 기내에서 어떤 엔터테인먼트를 제공했나요?

____

____

2. 추후 지속해서 업데이트할 서비스는 무엇인가요?

____

____

3. 김 씨가 경험한 기내 서비스를 요약하세요.

____

____

UNIT 10

In-flight Sales

Words and Phrases

Match the words with the sentences.

accept allowance liquor duty free
run out of change brand

1. We have many ____________ available. They are in the catalog.
2. Duty free ______________ is one bottle, sir.
3. We ____________ all major credit cards or you can pay cash.
4. What kinds of _______________ items do you sell in the cabin?
5. I'm afraid we have _______________ those items.
6. I'm sorry, I will bring your _______________ right away.
7. We have many ___________ items such as whisky, gin, vodka and brandy.

Useful Expressions

1. Would you like to buy any duty free items?
2. We are selling duty free items.
3. This guide will show you what we have.
4. This magazine has a list of our sales items
5. We've run out of Royal Salute.
6. I'm sorry, but all the Ballantine's 17 years have been sold out.
7. The total comes to 235 dollars altogether.
8. The total amount is 102 dollars.
9. Here's 17 dollars for your change.
10. The exchange rate in the cabin is 1,200 won to the dollar.
11. Only one bottle is allowed for duty free allowance.
12. Would you mind waiting until we have enough change?
13. I'm sorry, but I'm afraid we don't accept Canadian dollar.
14. Please print your name and passport number on the back of the cheque.
15. Would you please countersign here?
16. You can pay by cash and credit card together.
17. I'm sorry, but I'm afraid we don't accept debit card in the cabin.
18. Do you have any other currency, instead?
19. I'll bring back your change soon.
20. Due to transit airport regulation, liquid items more than 100m*l* are not allowed. What about buying duty free items on the next portion of your flight?
21. I'll put the liquid item more than 100m*l* in the transparent bag with the receipt. Please do not open it until you get the connecting flight.

22. You can pre-order duty free items for your return flight.

23. Please take your time and let us know when you decide what to buy.

24. I am not that sure that all the sales items in the cabin are cheaper than other duty free shops.

25. I'm sorry, but we have to stop the in-flight sales because the fasten seatbelt sign is on.

26. We can't sell anymore because we've already sealed and locked all the compartment for landing. We'll be landing very shortly.

27. We cannot sell anymore since we are preparing for landing. Your kind understanding would be appreciated.

Conversation

Read the dialogues below and practice speaking with your partner by taking turns.

Dialogue 1_ In-flight shopping

F/A : Would you like to buy any duty free items?
PAX : What kind of cosmetics do you have?
F/A : We have some basic skin make up products, and color make up cosmetics. You just can get more information through this in-flight sales magazine, sir.
PAX : Oh, thanks.
F/A : No problem. If you need anything to buy, just let me know.

Dialogue 2_ In-flight shopping guide

F/A : May I take your order for the duty free items?
PAX : What do you have?
F/A : This brochure has all the information about our duty free items, ma'am. Please take you time to look at it and let us know when you decide what to buy.
PAX : Okay.

Dialogue 3_ In-flight shopping assistance

PAX : Excuse me, Miss. I'd like to buy two bottles of Johnnie Walker Blue.
F/A : Certainly, sir. The total comes to ○○○ dollars.
PAX : Do you accept Canadian dollar?
F/A : I'm sorry, sir, but we don't accept Canadian dollar.
PAX : Okay. Then I'll pay by credit card.
F/A : Thank you, sir.

Dialogue 4_ In-flight shopping assistance

F/A : Excuse me, ma'am. Here is your order, one Chloé Eau de Toilette, and two Diorsnow UV shields. Is that correct?

PAX : Yes. I'll pay in US dollar. How much are these?

F/A : The total amount is 198 dollars.

PAX : Here's 200 dollars.

F/A : Thank you, ma'am. Here's your change 2 dollars.

Dialogue 5_ In-flight shopping assistance

PAX : I'd like to buy two bottles of Royal Salute.

F/A : I understand, sir. Where is your seat, sir?

PAX : 31A.

F/A : Would you please return to your seat, sir? (Would you please wait in your seat, sir?) We'll come to you very shortly.

PAX : Okay.

F/A : Thank you for your kind understanding.

Dialogue 6_ In-flight shopping assistance

F/A : Here's the chocolate and the Johnnie Walker Blue you ordered.

PAX : Oh, thanks. How much are these?

F/A : The total comes to 199 US dollars.

PAX : Can I use traveler's cheque?

F/A : Certainly, ma'am.

PAX : Here you are.

F/A : Thank you. Would you please countersign here and print your name and passport number on the back of the check?

PAX : Sure.

F/A : Thank you. Here's your change, one dollar.

Dialogue 7_ Items sold out

PAX : Excuse me, Miss. I'd like to buy three boxes of Godiva chocolate.

F/A : I'm very sorry, sir, but I'm afraid we've run out of Godiva chocolate today. Would you care for something else, instead? We have Lindt chocolate.

PAX : Okay. Then I'll buy three Lindt chocolates.

F/A : Sure, sir. Here are your chocolates. They are 108 dollars altogether.

PAX : I'll pay by credit card.

F/A : Certainly, sir. Thank you.

Dialogue 8_ Change unavailable

F/A : Excuse me, sir. We don't have enough change right now. Would you mind waiting until we have enough change? It won't be long.

PAX : Sure. Just don't forget, please.

F/A : Absolutely, sir. Thank you for your kind understanding.

Dialogue 9_ Receipt unavailable

PAX : Could you give me a cash receipt?

F/A : I'm sorry, but I'm afraid we can not issue the cash receipt on the flight due to related statute.

PAX : Oh, really? Then I'll pay by card.

F/A : Certainly, ma'am.

Dialogue 10_ In-flight shopping assistance

PAX : What kinds of duty free items do you sell?
F/A : You can see all the list of items in our in-flight sales catalog.
PAX : Good! I'd like to buy some liquor.
F/A : We have many brands available. They are in the front of the catalog.
PAX : How many bottles may I take to korea with me?
F/A : You are allowed to bring two bottles of liquor into Korea.
PAX : Thank you. Can I pay by Thai baht?
F/A : I'm very sorry, but I'm afraid we don't accept Thai baht. Do you have any other currency?
PAX : I have Japanese yen. Would it be OK?
F/A : Perfect, sir. Thank you.

ANNOUNCEMENT In-flight sales

Ladies and gentlemen, in a few minutes, we'll begin our sales of duty-free items.

If you'd like to purchase any items, please let us know as the duty-free sales cart passes by your seat.

We accept Korean won, U.S dollar, Japanese yen, chinese yuan, euro, and credit card.

The duty-free allowances for (Country Name) are ________ liter of liquor(s), ________ carton(s) of cigarettes and ________ ounce(s) of perfume.

For your convenience, we have a pre-order form which will allow you to order items and pick them up on your return flight.

For further information, please contact your flight attendants.

Thank you.

Phrases Tips

다음 구문을 활용해 다양한 문장을 만들어 보세요.

You can pay cash with + 국가의 화폐	You can pay cash with US dollar.
	You can pay cash with Korean won.
	You can pay cash with Japanese yen.
	You can pay cash with European euro.

I'm afraid	this item is all sold out today.
	it is only available by preordering.
	we don't accept that currency.
	we can't carry every product on short flight.
	I don't have enough change at the moment.

Activity

다음 문장을 이용하여 기내 대화를 만드세요.

1. Do you have any other currency, instead?

____

2. What about purchasing duty free items on the next portion of your flight?

____

3. I'm sorry, but we don't have enough change at this moment.

____

4. Please take your time and let us know when you decide what to buy.

____

5. I'm sorry, but we have to stop the in-flight sales because the fasten seatbelt sign is on.

____

6. I'm not sure that all the sales items in the cabin are cheaper than other duty free shops.

____

Reading Comprehension

다음을 읽고 물음에 답하세요.

Does In-flight Duty-free Sales Generate Sufficient Revenue?

Delta Air Lines has decided that the in-flight duty-free service is not valuable and has discontinued in-flight duty-free sales. However, industry experts forecast the airline duty-free sales to be a $3 billion global business with potential for further growth. Some successful airline programs generate annual profits of $100-200 million solely from duty-free sales. The opportunities for in-flight retail is not decreasing but rather increasing.

While Delta Air Lines may have deemed carrying duty-free items on board as not valuable, Korean Air conducts nearly $200 million in annual in-flight duty-free sales.

One of the reasons for the success of Korean Air's in-flight retail program lies here: there is an actual duty-free shop designed by Lancôme inside the A380. It is a real store equipped with items that visitors can browse. It offers cosmetics, perfumes, liquor, fashion items, pearls, health supplements, chocolates, watches, electronics, pens, and more. To create space for the Sky Shop, Korean Air had to remove 13 seats from the A380. It was a significant loss of potential revenue at a time when most airlines are trying to sell more seats. Korean Air fills the revenue lost from seat sales with duty-free sales. Sky Shop also ensures minimum revenue for all flights by gaining advertising profits from motion ads on the video walls of Sky Shop, product placements on display shelves, and ads behind the products.

Korean Air is one of the few major airlines that provide a cyber store, allowing passengers to pre-order duty-free items even before boarding the aircraft. The shopping site (CyberSkyShop.com) is available in various languages and has received top industry ratings. For example, the in-seat entertainment systems that were once used for watching movies or playing games have made ways for next-generation consoles that passengers can use for web searches, sending emails, ordering drinks, and selecting meal options. The IFEC console (similar to a smartphone) is equipped with a credit card reader, allowing passengers to complete the entire transaction from duty-free shopping to payment without the involvement of flight attendants.

1. 기내 면세품 판매를 중단한 항공사는 어디이며 그 이유는 무엇인가요?

____

____

2. 대한항공 기내 판매 매출이 증가한 요인은 무엇인가요?

____

____

3. 앞으로 발전할 기내 판매 방법은 무엇인가요?

____

____

UNIT 11

Cabin Check & Walking around

Words and Phrases

Match the words with the sentences.

call button　extra　pillow　cooperation
is not allowed　ahead of　courteous

1. If you need anything, please press this ________________ .
2. Could I have blanket and ________________ , please?
3. Smoking ____________________ on board during the flight.
4. Thank you very much for your ________________ .
5. Do you have ________________ meal that I can have? I'm still hungry.
6. The cabin crew is very ________________ to all passengers.
7. We will arrive in Korea ten minutes ____________________ time.

Useful Expressions

1. Can I help you?
2. May I turn off the call button?
3. Would you like a pillow?
4. How do you feel now?
5. How about something hot to drink?
6. I'll check the cabin temperature.
7. Would you like me to turn on the reading light?
8. I'll bring it for you right away.
9. I'll check if there is any blanket left.
10. All the lavatories are occupied now.
11. The seatbelt sign has been turned on. Please fasten your seatbelt.
12. Would you please fasten your seatbelt for your safety?
13. Are you having trouble sleeping?
14. I'm sorry, but would you please have your children calm down a little bit as a courtesy to other passengers who are sleeping?
15. Would you please close your window shade? Most of the passengers are taking a rest now. May I turn on the reading light for you?
16. Would you please fasten your seatbelt because an unexpected change in the air stream can cause turbulence during the flight?
17. We are experiencing turbulence now. Would you please return to your seat and fasten your seatbelt?

Conversation

Read the dialogues below and practice speaking with your partner by taking turns.

Dialogue 1_ Cabin temperature

PAX : Excuse me, Miss. It's really cold in here. Could you do something for me?

F/A : I'm so sorry, ma'am. I'll check the cabin temperature. And may I bring a blanket and a cup of hot water for you?

PAX : Yes, please. That would be nice.

......

F/A : Here's your blanket and hot water.

PAX : Thanks.

F/A : My pleasure. Also I raised the temperature in the cabin, but it will take a few minutes for cabin to heat up.

PAX : Thanks.

......

F/A : Excuse me, ma'am. How do you feel now?

PAX : I feel much better.

F/A : I'm glade to hear that. Is there anything else I can do for you?

PAX : I'm fine. Thank you.

F/A : I hope you enjoy your flight.

Dialogue 2_ Passenger who seats next to the galley

F/A : Excuse me, sir. I'm afraid you're hearing the noise from the galley. If there is anything I can do for you, please don't hesitate to push this call button.

PAX : Thanks.

Dialogue 3_ Missing order

PAX : Hello, Miss.

F/A : Yes, sir? How can I help you?

PAX : I asked someone else for a cup of coffee 10minutes ago, but she didn't bring it to me. I guess she forgot it.

F/A : Oh, I'm very sorry. I'll bring it to you right away.

PAX : Okay. Please don't make me wait too long.

F/A : Certainly, sir. It won't be long.

......

Here's your coffee and some cookies, sir. I'm sorry again to have kept you waiting too long.

PAX : That' okay.

Dialogue 4_ Screen problem

F/A : Sir, how can I help you?

PAX : I think there is a problem with my screen.

F/A : Doesn't it work?

PAX : Actually it was working for a bit, but suddenly it turned off.

F/A : Really? Did you try to turn it on again?

PAX : Yes, but it didn't work.

F/A : Let me take a look... there seems to be a problem with the screen.

PAX : Can you fix it?

F/A : I'm very sorry, but I can't fix it now. Why don't you move to another seat? There are some empty seats in the front of the cabin today.

PAX : Okay. Just let me know where I should sit.

F/A : Yes, sir. Please follow me. I'm sorry again for this inconvenience.

Dialogue 5_ Passenger who wants to see first class

F/A : Excuse me, ma'am. May I help you?

PAX : I just want to look around the first class section.

F/A : I'm sorry, but the first class passengers are taking a rest right now and shouldn't be disturbed. If you'd like to, I'll show you after landing.

PAX : Okay.

F/A : Thank you for your kind understanding.

Dialogue 6_ Noisy children

PAX1 : Excuse me, Miss. I really want to sleep during the flight, but that little boy is continuously making noise. Could you do something about it?

F/A : Yes, ma'am. I'll see what I can do.

......

(to PAX2) Excuse me, ma'am. I'm sorry, but some of other passengers would like to take some rest. Could you please have your son be a little quieter for a while? I really appreciate your cooperation.

Dialogue 7_ Passenger who wants to get into the cockpit

PAX : Excuse me, Miss. My son wants to see the cockpit. Would that be possible?

F/A : I'm very sorry, sir. Passengers are not allowed to get into the cockpit during the flight for the security reasons.

PAX : Okay. I see.

F/A : Thank you for your understanding.

Dialogue 8_ Passenger with a baby

F/A : Excuse me, ma'am. Would you please hold your baby outside the seatbelt? That will be more comfortable and safer for your baby.

PAX : Oh, I see. And do you have a diaper? I think I need some more diaper during the flight.

F/A : Yes, we do. I'll bring some soon.

PAX : Thank you very much.

F/A : It's my pleasure.

Dialogue 9_ Arrival time

PAX : How long will it be before[1] we get to New York?

F/A : We expect to arrive in about two hours. We are about 20 minutes ahead of schedule.[2]

PAX : Thanks.

F/A : No problem.

Alternative Expressions

1. How many hours will it be before
   How much longer will it be before
2. We'll be arriving approximately 20 minutes ahead of schedule.
   We are a little behind schedule.

Dialogue 10_ Time remaining to destination

PAX : Excuse me, Miss. How many more hours to London?

F/A : There are 3 more hours remaining.

PAX : What's the time difference between London and Seoul?

F/A : London is 9 hours behind Seoul.

PAX : Thanks.

F/A : My pleasure.

Phrases Tips

다음 구문을 활용해 다양한 문장을 만들어 보세요.

I'm so sorry	for the inconvenience.
	to have kept you waiting too long.

Passengers are not	allowed to get into the cockpit.
	permitted to smoke on airplanes.

for a + (시간, 정도를 나타내는) 명사	for a while
	for a bit
	for a few minutes
	for a short time

ANNOUNCEMENT Distributing entry documents

Ladies and gentlemen, our cabin crew will be handling out entry documents for entering into Korea.

Non Korean citizens must complete both an arrival card and customs form.

Only one customs form is required per family.

Today's date is (Month / Date), and this is __________ flight __________ .

Please notify your cabin crew if you need any information or assistance.

We will be happy to assist you.

Activity

다음 기내 대화를 완성하세요.

F/A : Sir, ______________ help you?

PAX : I think there is a problem with my screen.

F/A : __________________ ?

PAX : Actually it was working for a while, but suddenly it turned off.

F/A : Really? Did you try ______________ again?

PAX : Yes, but it didn't work.

F/A : Let me ______________ there _________ be a problem with the screen.

PAX : Can you ____________ it?

F/A : I'm very sorry, but I can't fix it now. Why don't you ______________ seat? There are some empty seats in the front of the cabin today.

PAX : Okay. Just let me know where I should sit.

F/A : Yes, sir. Please follow me. I'm ______________________________________

PAX1 : Excuse me, Miss. I really want to sleep during the flight, but that little boy is continuously making noise. Could you do something about it?

F/A : ______________________________

......

(to PAX2) Excuse me, ma'am.

I'm sorry, ____

Could you ____ ?

I really appreciate your cooperation.

Reading Comprehension

다음을 읽고 물음에 답하세요.

Types of "Problematic Passengers"

A passenger with a huge build placed a large piece of luggage in the aisle and said, "Lift it up!" I politely asked for help in lifting it since it seemed too heavy. Suddenly, he got angry and shouted, "What do you even know how to do?" All the other passengers looked at us, making the situation uncomfortable. I apologized for the inconvenience caused and explained that the passenger was upset because the seats were too narrow to sit. After apologizing again and empathizing with his concerns, he finally found his seat and settled down.

As soon as a passenger boarded the economy class, he took off his jacket and demanded that it be stored in the first-class coatroom, claiming it was an expensive luxury item. When I explained that it was against the regulations and not possible, he insisted on having the first-class meal brought to him since he can't eat the economy class meal due to his picky tastes. Despite it being prohibited by the onboard regulations, he continued to get angry and persistently made the request. I apologized and explained that there were no leftover first-class meals available. In response, he threatened to file a complaint with the company and demanded that I bring him the necessary paperwork. It was an exhausting flight.

I felt a strange sensation near my chest, where I was selling duty-free items on board. When I turned around, I realized that a male passenger was touching my chest. I sternly said, "What are you doing?" but instead of feeling remorse, he responded loudly, "I just wanted to see the girl's name, why are you getting angry about this?" and even laughed with another man sitting next to him. I felt humiliated and my body trembled with embarrassment.

Once, a passenger refused to show his boarding pass, saying, "I already showed it at the gate, why are you bothering me again?" and ended up punching the flight attendant in the face. What's even more absurd is that they allowed such a passenger to board and even let him reach his destination. Assaulting flight attendants is an unforgivable act and should be strictly dealt with to the fullest extent of the law.

1. 첫째 사례의 내용은 무엇인가요?

____

____

2. 일등석 식사를 요구한 승객의 마지막 행동은 무엇인가요?

____

____

3. 셋째 사례와 넷째 사례의 내용은 각각 무엇인가요?

____

____

PART

3

Service before Landing

UNIT 12

Entry Card Distribution

Words and Phrases

Match the words with the sentences.

entry documents	final destination	customs form
permanent	declare	transit	capital letters

1. You have to ______________ them on the customs declaration form.
2. Are you a visitor or a ______________ resident?
3. Is Korea your ______________________ ?
4. You only need to fill out one ______________________ per family.
5. Please write your name in ______________________ .
6. You must complete these ______________________ to enter Japan.
7. Are you going to ______________ at Incheon International Airport?

Useful Expressions

1. Would you please fill out entry document?
2. Where is your final destination?
3. Only one customs form is needed per family.
4. Each passenger must complete the entry card separately.
5. Even if you have nothing to declare, you still need to fill out the customs form.
6. Do you have anything to declare?
7. Do you have a valid visa or ESTA for the purpose of your visit?
8. Are you a U.S. citizen or a resident?
9. You don't need to fill out the entry card.
10. Please write it in English capital letters.
11. Please write your address in U.S. here.
12. May I help you with it?
13. What is your native country?
14. Where did you get your visa?
15. Let me check if your entry card is filled in properly.
16. All passengers must complete the quarantine form on this flight for entering (Country Name).
17. It is strictly prohibited to bring fruit into (Country Name). If you have any fruit, I would like to suggest you dispose of it in the cabin before landing.

Conversation

Read the dialogues below and practice speaking with your partner by taking turns.

Dialogue 1_ Entry document

F/A : Excuse me, ma'am. Here is your arrival card for Korea.
PAX : Do I have to fill this out?
F/A : Are you visiting Korea or do you live in Korea?
PAX : I'm traveling with my family.
F/A : Then you have to fill out the entry card.
PAX : Okay. Do you have any pen?
F/A : Here you are. And you also need to complete customs form. Here's your customs form.
PAX : Thank you.
F/A : No problem.

Dialogue 2_ Customs form

PAX : Excuse me, Miss. What's the duty free limit entering Korea?
F/A : two bottles of whisky, 60ml of perfume, and a carton of cigarettes are allowed tax free.
PAX : Thanks. I'm traveling with my family. Should each of us fill out the customs form?
F/A : No, sir. You can complete just one customs form for your family. [1]
PAX : Oh, I see.
F/A : If you need any assistance filling out the form, please let me know.

Alternative Expressions

1. Only one customs form is needed per family.

Dialogue 3_ Transit passenger

PAX : Excuse me, Miss. I'm going to stay in Seoul for a couple of hours and take the city tour. Then I'll fly on to Singapore tonight. Do I have to complete the entry document?

F/A : Yes, sir. You should fill out the form and write 'TRANSIT' here where it asks you about your purpose of travel.

PAX : Thanks.

F/A : It's my pleasure.

Dialogue 4_ Transit passenger

PAX : Hello, can I ask something?

F/A : Absolutely, ma'am. How can I help you?

PAX : I'm a transit passenger, and I'm going to stay at the Incheon Airport for several hours. Do I have to fill out the entry form?

F/A : No, ma'am. You don't have to fill out the form. (If you don't leave the transit area, the entry documents are not necessary, ma'am.)
Is there anything else you want to ask?

PAX : No, Miss. Thanks.

F/A : My pleasure.

Dialogue 5_ Residents entering USA

PAX : Excuse me. I live in the United States, but I'm not a U.S. citizen. Do I have to complete this card?

F/A : Do you have an alien registration card?

PAX : Yes, I do.

F/A : Then you only have to fill out the customs form.

PAX : I got it. Thanks.

F/A : No problem.

Dialogue 6_ Tourists entering USA

PAX : Excuse me. I'm just tourist. Do I have to fill out these forms?
F/A : Yes, ma'am. All the passengers except U.S. citizens, residents, immigrants to the United States and Canadian must complete the entry card and customs form.

Dialogue 7_ Traveling in group

PAX : I'm traveling in a group. Should each of us fill out an entry form individually?
F/A : Yes, ma'am. Each passenger must complete the entry card separately.
PAX : I'm traveling with my family. Should we complete these forms separately?
F/A : Each of your family members should fill out the entry card, but one customs form is enough for your family.
PAX : Okay. Thank you.
F/A : No problem.

ANNOUNCEMENT Entry documents for entering Korea

Ladies and gentlemen, for entering Korea, please have your passport and other documents ready.

If you are carrying any items valued over the duty free allowance or more than __________ US dollars or the equivalent in foreign currency, you must declare it on the customs form.

If you are carrying any kind of fruit, plant, or meat products, they must be declared on the customs form and be quranted.

Passengers who have baggage arriving on another aircraft or by ship must fill out two customs forms.

For further details, please contact a flight attendant.

Thank you.

Phrases Tips

다음 구문을 활용해 다양한 문장을 만들어 보세요.

You need to	fill out these forms.
	fasten your seatbelt.
	complete an arrival card.

Are you	a permanent resident of Korea?
	traveling with any family members?

Do you have	an alien registration card?
	a valid visa for the purpose of your visit?

Activity

다음 기내 대화를 완성하세요.

PAX : Hello, can I ask something?

F/A : Absolutely, ma'am. ______________________________________

____?

PAX : I'm a transit passenger, and I'm going to stay at the Incheon Airport for several hours. Do I have to fill out the entry form?

F/A : ____________________________________

(____)

Is there anything else you want to ask?

PAX : No, Miss. Thanks.

F/A : My pleasure.

PAX : Excuse me, Miss. What's the duty free limit entering ________ ?

F/A : ___ bottles of whisky, ____ oz of perfume, and ____ cartons of cigarette are allowed tax free.

PAX : Thanks. I'm traveling with my family. Should each of us fill out the customs form?

F/A : ______________________________________ for your family.

(____)

PAX : Oh, I see.

F/A : If you need ____________________________, please let me know.

Reading Comprehension

다음을 읽고 물음에 답하세요.

Information on U.S. Immigration Documents

Passengers traveling to the United States no longer need to fill out paper immigration forms upon entry. The paper form I-94, which serves as proof of legal status and duration of stay in the United States, has been replaced by an electronic automated entry and exit system. This eliminates the need to fill out the paper form on board during entry to the U.S. and retain it until departure.

The transition to the electronic system reduces the time required for the immigration process upon entry and eliminates the hassle of completing paperwork on board. It also prevents situations that arise from losing or incorrectly filling out the forms, as they can now be completed electronically.

U.S. entry requirements: Recent travel restrictions explained.
As of 2023, the COVID-19 vaccine requirement for passengers traveling to the U.S. has been lifted, meaning that those who have not been vaccinated or partially vaccinated can enter the U.S. without restrictions. However, a valid passport and ESTA visa are still required for entry. In fact, until recently, the U.S. had made it mandatory for all non-resident foreigners to be vaccinated in their home country before entering the U.S. However, on May 12, they announced that entry is possible regardless of vaccination status.

This applies to all travelers entering the U.S. by air or land. What COVID test is required? Generally, the U.S. does not require a COVID test before travel. However, restrictions may vary when traveling elsewhere, so please check. For example, in early 2023, the U.S. introduced temporary testing requirements for those coming from or transiting through China. *Can you travel to the U.S. without an ESTA?* All travelers require a visa or visa waiver (known as ESTA; the latter must be applied for at least three days before travel).

1. I-94 입국서류는 무엇으로 대체되었나요?

____

____

2. 2023년에 5월에 발표한 내용은 무엇인가요?

____

____

3. 미국 입국 시 꼭 필요한 것은 무엇인가요?

____

____

UNIT 13

Preparation for Landing

Words and Phrases

Match the words with the sentences.

uninstall　landing　collect　securely

annoucement　remain　Air traffic congestion

1. We have to ______________ your baby bassinet to prepare for landing.
2. There will be an ______________ to prepare for landing soon.
3. I'm afraid we must ______________ the headphones now.
4. Please ______________ in your seat until the seatbelt sign is turned off.
5. We will be ______________ at Incheon International Airport.
6. Please make sure your seatbelt is ______________ fastened.
7. ___________________ caused delays around Korea.

Useful Expression

1. Would you please fasten your seatbelt?
2. May I have(take) your headphones please?
3. Would you please open your window shade?
4. We'll have good weather in Seoul.
5. Would you please return to your seat and fasten your seatbelt?
6. Would you please return your seatback to the upright position?

Conversation

Read the dialogues below and practice speaking with your partner by taking turns.

Dialogue 1_ Collecting headphones

F/A : Excuse me, sir. May I have your headphones? We will be landing soon.

PAX : I put them in the seat pocket.

F/A : I see them. Thanks.

ANNOUNCEMENT Collecting headphones

Ladies and gentlemen, we hope you have enjoyed our entertainment program.

Our flight attendants will collect your headphones shortly.

Your cooperation is much appreciated.

Thank you.

Dialogue 2_ Safety check

F/A : Excuse me, ma'am. Could you please fasten your seatbelt and return your seatback to the upright position? (Would you please close your tray table and open your window shade?) We will be landing shortly.

PAX : Okay.

F/A : Thank you.

ANNOUNCEMENT Preparing for landing

Ladies and gentlemen, we're now making our decent into ○○○ International Airport.

Please return your seat and fasten your seatbelt.

And return your seatback and tray table to the upright position.

We would like to ask you to open the window shade nearest you.

Please make sure your bags are stowed in the overhead bins or under the seat.

All electronic devices such as personal computers, CD players and electronic games should be turned off.

Thank you.

Dialogue 3_ Safety check

F/A : Excuse me, ma'am. We'll be landing very shortly. Would you please return to your seat and fasten your seatbelt?

PAX : Okay.

F/A : Thank you, ma'am.

Dialogue 4_ Bassinet down

F/A : Excuse me, ma'am. We'll be landing shortly. May I take the bassinet down?

PAX : Sure, please.

......

F/A : Please hold your baby outside your seatbelt. It is much safer for your baby.

PAX : Oh, I see.

Dialogue 5_ Baggage check

F/A : Excuse me, ma'am. Would you please put your bag in the overhead bin or under the seat in front of you? We will be landing soon.

PAX : Do I have to? I'd like to keep my bag close by.

F/A : I'm sorry, ma'am, but we have to keep the aisle clear during landing. It's for your safety.

PAX : Okay.

F/A : Thank you, ma'am.

Dialogue 6_ Baggage check

PAX : Excuse me, Miss. Would you bring me the bag I gave you earlier?

F/A : Sir, may I bring your bag after landing? It's much safer for you. I won't forget to bring your bag to you.

PAX : Okay.

F/A : Thank you.

Dialogue 7_ Collecting used cup

F/A : Excuse me, ma'am. Are you finished with your drink? We will be landing shortly.

PAX : Yes, but can I have another drink?

F/A : I'm very sorry, ma'am. We've closed all the compartment for landing. So I can get you only water at this moment. Would that be alright?

PAX : Oh, that would be nice. Thank you.

Dialogue 8_ Landing delayed

F/A : We're very sorry, ma'am. But we are not able to land at the scheduled time due to dense fog over the Incheon Airport. We'll be holding for about 30 minutes, and we'll keep you informed.

PAX : Okay, I see.

F/A : Thank you for your understanding.

Dialogue 9_ Landing delayed

PAX : Miss, are we landing now?

F/A : Yes, we are. But there's going to be a slight delay.

PAX : Why?

F/A : The bad weather caused delay around the airport area. So there are several planes ahead of us.

PAX : How long do we wait more?

F/A : We'll be landing about 20 minutes behind schedule. The captain will make an announcement.

PAX : I see.

F/A : Thank you for your understanding.

Dialogue 10_ Local weather

PAX : What's the weather like in Los Angeles?

F/A : It's cloudy with a temperature of 32 degrees Fahrenheit.

Dialogue 11_ Transportation

PAX : Excuse me, Miss. How can I get to the downtown from the airport?
F/A : There are various public transportation. You can take a taxi or airport bus or subway.
PAX : How long does it take to get the downtown by taxi?
F/A : It takes about one and half hours. It depends on the traffic.
PAX : Thanks.
F/A : My pleasure, ma'am. I hope you like Seoul.

ANNOUNCEMENT Transit procedure

Ladies and gentlemen, for those passengers with a connecting domestic flight, please pick up all checked baggage and clear customs here at Incheon International Airport.

Please move to the domestic check-in counter either at Incheon International Airport or at your arrival at Gimpo Airport.

When you pick up your baggage, please check that your baggage tag number and claim tag match correctly.

Passengers with connecting international flight, please follow the guidance of our ground staff.

Thank you.

ANNOUNCEMENT Landing

Ladies and gentlemen, we're now making our final approach.

Please make sure your seatbelt is fastened.

Also, recheck that your seatback is in the upright position and your tray table is closed.

Thank you.

Phrases Tips

다음 구문을 활용해 다양한 문장을 만들어 보세요.

soon과 비슷한 표현 곧 머지않아	
	shortly
	anytime now
	before long
	in no time
	sometime soon

a pair of + 명사 복수형 한 쌍의 ~	
	a pair of headphones
	a pair of slippers
	a pair of earplugs
	a pair of socks
	a pair of shoes

Activity

착륙을 준비 중일 때 다음 상황에 맞게 기내 대화를 만드세요.

1. 승객의 짐이 복도에 나와 있을 때

2. baby-bassinet을 사용한 승객에게

3. 음료를 더 요청하는 승객에게

Reading Comprehension

다음을 읽고 물음에 답하세요.

The Importance of Cabin Crew in the Landing and Take-off Procedures

Cabin crew members have a crucial list of tasks to be performed on every flight for safety reasons. Tasks such as safety equipment checks and pre-flight inspections must be completed without fail. Take-off and landing are critical phases of the flight for cabin crew, and it is important to ensure that the cabin is completely secure. This includes checking if passengers have securely fastened their seatbelts, if seatbacks and tray tables are in the upright position, and if window shades are open. Most importantly, a final check should be done to ensure that there are no items near the emergency exits that could obstruct emergency evacuations. Once all safety checks are completed, the cabin crew members also take their seats.

After cabin crew members are seated and have fastened their seatbelts on the jump seats, they have another task known as the 30-second review. This review, conducted for 30 seconds, helps cabin crew members anticipate and correctly perform unplanned emergency situations and evacuations. The time just before landing and after take-off is used for emergency training, procedures, and familiarizing cabin crew members with their duties and responsibilities.

A few years ago, there was a case of an emergency evacuation due to an engine fire just before take-off at the Haneda International Airport in Japan. A passenger plane bound for Gimpo Airport from Tokyo Haneda Airport experienced a fire in the left engine during take-off preparations. The aircraft had a total of 319 people on board, including 302 passengers and 17 crew members. The airport authorities and Japanese fire fighting authorities promptly dispatched around 60 fire trucks, as well as over 100 firefighters and police riot squad members, to extinguish the fire. Some passengers sustained minor injuries while evacuating through the emergency slides.

Aircraft doors are equipped with 'slides' for emergency evacuations, and cabin crew members receive annual emergency evacuation training. Thanks to the cabin crew's emergency evacuation training, all passengers were able to evacuate safely.

1. 승무원이 이행해야 하는 착륙 준비 업무는 무엇인가요?

____

____

2. 승무원이 좌석에 착석한 후에 해야 하는 행동은 무엇인가요?

____

____

3. 비상 탈출을 하게 된 이유는 무엇인가요?

____

____

PART 4

Landing Tasks in the Cabin

UNIT 14

Deplane

Words and Phrases

Match the words with the sentences.

deplane parking area completely

assistance pleasant belongings refrain

1. Please remain seated until the aircraft stops ____________ .

2. We haven't reached ______________ yet.

3. Don't forget to bring your ____________ with you.

4. please refrain from using mobile phone until you ____________ .

5. Would you like an ____________ with your bag?

6. Did you have __________ flight with us today?

7. You may now ____________ through the front door.

Useful Expression

1. We haven't reached the parking area yet.
2. Would you please remain seated until we reach the parking area?
3. Thank you for flying with us.
4. I hope to see you on board again.
5. Have a nice stay in Honolulu.
6. I hope you have a great time in Seoul.

Conversation

Read the dialogues below and practice speaking with your partner by taking turns.

Dialogue 1_ During taxiing

F/A : Excuse me, sir. We've not reached the parking area. Would you please remain seated until the plane comes to a complete stop at the parking area?

PAX : Alright.

F/A : Thank you.

Dialogue 2_ During taxiing

F/A : Would you please wait until after the aircraft comes to a complete stop to take out your baggage from the overhead bin?

PAX : Okay.

F/A : Thank you for your cooperation.

Dialogue 3_ Returning bag

F/A : Excuse me, ma'am. Here's your bag you gave me before take-off.

PAX : Oh, thanks.

F/A : You're welcome. Please make sure that you have all your personal belongings.

Dialogue 4_ Upper deck PAX deplane

F/A : Excuse me, sir. May I ask you to wait here while the passengers in the upper deck are coming down? Your cooperation will be appreciated.

PAX : Okay, I see.

Dialogue 5_ Saying good bye

F/A : Did you enjoy the flight with us today?
PAX : Absolutely.
F/A : Thank you. I hope to see you on board again.

Dialogue 6_ Farewell

F/A : Was everything alright, ma'am? It's been a pretty long flight.
PAX : I had a good time during the flight. Thanks.
F/A : I am so glad to hear that, ma'am. I hope to see you again. Have a great time in Seoul.

ANNOUNCEMENT Farewell

Ladies and gentlemen, it's our pleasure to welcome you to _________ International Airport.

The local time (here in _____) is ____ A.M/P.M (on ______)

For your safety, please keep your seatbelt fastened until the captain turns off the seatbelt sign.

Also, refrain from using mobile phone until you deplane.

When opening the overhead bins, please be careful of contents that may have moved during the flight.

Before leaving the aircraft, please check that there are no items left in your seat pocket or under your seat.

Please take all carry-on baggage with you when you deplane.

On behalf of the entire crew, we've enjoyed serving you today and we hope to see you soon.

Thank you.

Phrases Tips

다음 구문을 활용해 다양한 문장을 만들어 보세요.

승객 하기 시 인사 표현	Thank you for flying with us.
	We thank you for flying with ○○○ Airlines.
	We hope to see you again soon.
	We look forward to meeting you again.
	Good bye for now.

It looks like (that) It seems like (that) ~인 것 같다	you are ready to deplane now.
	we will land soon.
	you need some help with your bag.
	we will delay due to bad weather.
	the turbulence will end shortly.

Activity

다음을 영작하세요.

1. 비행은 즐거우셨습니까?

   ____

2. 서울에서 즐거운 시간 보내시기 바랍니다.

   ____

3. 다시 만나 뵙기를 바랍니다.

   ____

4. 시내까지 가는 다양한 대중 교통편이 있습니다.

   ____

5. 잊으신 물건이 없는지 다시 한번 확인하시기 바랍니다.

   ____

6. 항공기가 완전히 멈출 때까지 좌석에 앉아 계시기 바랍니다.

   ____

7. 입국에 필요한 서류를 준비하시기 바랍니다.

   ____

8. 2층의 승객들께서 하기할 때까지 잠시만 기다려 주시겠습니까?

   ____

Reading Comprehension

다음을 읽고 물음에 답하세요.

A Man Who Opened the Aircraft Door in Mid-air, Terrifying the Passengers

Recently, an incident occurred where the emergency exit door of an Asiana Airlines plane opened just before landing at Daegu Airport. The man sitting in the emergency exit seat forcibly opened the emergency exit door in mid-air, claiming that he felt suffocated and wanted to get off quickly. As the emergency exit door was forcefully opened, causing a rush of wind inside the cabin, the passengers on board the plane were terrified. A total of 200 people, including the crew, were on board, and they remained terrified until they disembarked. Among them, 9 people showed symptoms of respiratory distress and received treatment at a hospital.

Furthermore, an incident of unruly behavior of a passenger occurred on a Jeju Air flight. According to the statements from passengers on the Jeju Air flight from Jeju to Incheon Airport, one passenger caused a disturbance on board after an hour from take-off and attempted to open the emergency exit. At an altitude of over 10,000 feet, the door cannot be opened manually due to the pressure difference. A Jeju Air representative confirmed the occurrence of the in-flight disturbance and stated that the crew had been monitoring the passenger closely as he had appeared unwell prior to causing the disturbance.

A similar incident also took place in the United States on an American Airlines flight. In this case, a male passenger attempted to break a champagne bottle and threatened the crew of the front of the aircraft with a plastic knife tucked into his shirt sleeve. He also pushed a cart into a flight attendant and kicked her. Subsequently, the passenger forcibly tried to open the front door of the plane with both hands, but the flight attendant swiftly subdued the passenger by striking his head with a coffee pot.

Coincidentally, a police officer who happened to be on board the flight apprehended the male passenger and dragged him down to the floor, using cable ties and tape to restrain his hands and feet. With the increasing frequency of such in-flight disturbances, concerns about safety and security incidents are growing, necessitating heightened vigilance and prioritization of safety by the cabin crew.

1. 대구 공항에서 사건이 발생한 이유는 무엇인가요?

____

____

2. 제주항공에서 어떤 사건이 발생했나요?

____

____

3. 미국 항공사 승무원들은 어떻게 대처했나요?

____

____

UNIT 15

Sick Passenger

Words and Phrases

Match the words with the sentences.

medicine　　throw up　　air sickness

allergic　　fainted　　heart attack　　first aid kit

1. A passenger ________________ and won't wake up.
2. Let me get you some medicine for _____________ .
3. Could I have some ____________ that I can take?
4. The passenger seems to have a ________________ .
5. My face is pale. I feel like I'm going to ________________ .
6. Are you _____________ to any medicine?
7. For emergency patients, there is a ________________ in the cabin.

Useful Expression

1. How do you feel now?
2. Are you allergic to any kind of medicine?
3. I hope you feel better soon.
4. I'm glad to see you're doing better.
5. I'll check if we have empty row available.
6. Have you ever had a bad reaction to any medicine?
7. I need to take your temperature.
8. Can I take your blood pressure?
9. Have you ever had this type of problem before?
10. Have you ever had these symptoms before?
11. Can I ask you something about your medical history?

Conversation

Read the dialogues below and practice speaking with your partner by taking turns.

Dialogue 1_ Ears pop

PAX : Excuse me, Miss.
F/A : Yes, ma'am. May I help you?
PAX : My ears are plugged up. Do you have anything for that?
F/A : Well, not really, ma'am. But you could try this. Hold your nose shut (like this) and blow out gently with your mouth closed.
PAX : Oh, that worked. Thank you.
F/A : You're welcome, ma'am. Can I get you anything else?

Dialogue 2_ Nauseous

PAX : Excuse me, Miss. I'm not feeling very well.
F/A : Oh, I'm sorry to hear that. How can I help you?
PAX : I feel nauseous. Do you have anything for that?
F/A : We have Alka-Seltzer and Pepto-Bismol.
PAX : Can I have some Pepto-Bismol?
F/A : Sure. I'll be right back.
......
Here you are. I hope you feel better soon.
......
How do you feel now?
PAX : I feel much better. Thanks.
F/A : I am happy to hear that. If there is anything I can get for you, just let me know, ma'am.

Dialogue 3_ Headache

PAX : Excuse me, Miss. I have a bad headache. Do you have any medicine for headache?

F/A : Oh, I am sorry to hear that. We have Tylenol for headache. Are you allergic to any medicine?

PAX : No, I'm not.

F/A : Yes, sir. I'll bring it to you right away. Would you like to take one or two tablets?

PAX : I think I need two tablets.

......

F/A : Here you are. I hope you feel better soon.

Dialogue 4_ Air sickness

PAX : Excuse me, Miss. I feel like vomiting. Is there anything for this?

F/A : Here's a airsickness bag. Please use this bag if you need to. And we have Bonaring-A for airsick. Would you like to take that medicine?

PAX : Yes, please.

F/A : Do you have any allergies to any medicine?

PAX : No. I don't.

F/A : Then I will bring it to you.

......

Here you are. I hope you get well soon.

Dialogue 5_ Indigestion

PAX : Excuse me, do you have any medicine for indigestion?

F/A : We have Bestase for indigestion. It is a Korean brand. Under your responsibility, we may provide you this first aid medicine. Would you like to try it?

PAX : Yes, please.

F/A : Certainly, sir. One moment, please.

......

Here you are.

PAX : Thanks.

F/A : No problem. I hope you feel better soon.

Dialogue 6_ Suffocation

PAX : Excuse me, Miss!

F/A : May I help you?

PAX : Yes, please. My wife is having difficulty breathing.

F/A : Just a moment, please. I'll page a doctor for you.

ANNOUNCEMENT Doctor paging

Ladies and gentlemen, may I have your attention, please?

We have a passenger in the cabin who needs special attention from a doctor or nurse. If there is a doctor or nurse in the cabin, please let one of the flight attendants know.

Thank you.

Phrases Tips

다음 구문을 활용해 다양한 문장을 만들어 보세요.

have difficulty + ~ing have trouble + ~ing ~하는 데 어려움을 겪다	My wife is having difficulty breathing.
	I have difficulty studying English Everyday.
	They have some trouble looking for a solution.

Activity

다음 증상에 대한 기내 대화를 만드세요.

nausea / cold / sore throat / indigestion / upset stomach

heartburn / diarrhea / air sickness / cough

Reading Comprehension

다음을 읽고 물음에 답하세요.

Flight Attendants' Duties in Case of In-flight Patients

There are cases where in-flight patients suddenly become ill. When a patient becomes ill, the crew, the purser, and the captain should be informed first, and if there is a doctor on board, s/he should be called upon depending on the patient's condition. If there is a doctor, s/he should be made aware of the situation and take appropriate measures and make every effort to ensure that the patient is stabilized.

In addition, the patient's symptoms should be identified, any appropriate treatment and stabilization efforts should be performed using medical equipment on board, and emergency treatment should be carried out according to the symptoms.

On a flight departing from the Incheon International Airport to Singapore, an announcement suddenly came on: "An emergency patient has occurred on board. If there is a medical professional among the passengers, please present your identification card and inform our crew." A male passenger in his 40s showed symptoms of respiratory distress and lost consciousness. The passenger said he had undergone heart surgery and had been on dialysis. The purser who learned of the patient's symptoms immediately informed the captain of the emergency situation, and the captain searched for medical personnel among the passengers through the in-flight announcement and consulted a university hospital via satellite phone.

One passenger who identified himself as a doctor came forward, and fortunately, there was also a flight attendant who had a nursing license. The two of them worked together, using onboard emergency oxygen masks and emergency medical kits (EMK) to provide oxygen to the patient and administer emergency treatment.

Upon hearing opinions that the patient's condition seemed critical, the captain diverted the flight to the Ho Chi Minh City Airport. The patient was then transferred to a hospital by the medical team waiting in Ho Chi Minh City. One of the most challenging tasks for cabin crew members is dealing with in-flight medical emergencies. When a patient arises, it can be extremely stressful and difficult to handle. However, both the flight attendants and the medical team must prioritize the safety and health of the patient and respond actively according to the situation.

1. 기내 환자 발생 시 가장 먼저 해야 할 일은 무엇인가요?

____

____

2. 기내에 의료진이 있는지 어떻게 확인하나요?

____

____

3. 싱가포르행 기내 환자는 어떠한 질병이 있었나요?

____

____

PART

5

Miscellaneous

1. In-flight Service Terms

1	aboard	If someone is aboard, he or she is on or in a vehicle such as a bus, train, ship, or airplane.
2	account for	To account for something is to take responsibility for or to give a reason for something.
3	air taxi	An air taxi is a charter passenger aircraft which operates on an on-demand basis.
4	air traffic control	Air traffic control is a system of equipment and staff who control and monitor air traffic.
5	air traffic	Air traffic refers to the number and movement of aircraft in the sky.
6	air vent	An air vent is a hole or space that lets in fresh air.
7	aircraft	Aircraft refers to any machine that is able to fly.
8	airline	An airline is a company that operates commercial air transportation.
9	aisle	An aisle is the passage that runs through the center of an aircraft to allow passengers to get to their seats.
10	allergic reaction	An allergic reaction is a sensitivity to a substance that comes in contact with the body.
11	allow	To allow is to permit something.
12	altitude	Altitude is height in relation to ground or sea level.
13	announce	To announce something is to make it known publicly, or to give notice to a group.
14	approach	An approach is the final path followed by an aircraft as it's landing.
15	approved	If something is approved, it is acceptable.
16	armrest	Armrests are the part of the chair that supports the arms.

17	baggage handler	A baggage handler transfers passengers' luggage from the airport to the plane.
18	baggage	Baggage includes bags, trunks, or suitcases used for traveling.
19	beneath	If something is beneath, it is directly under something else, or in a lower position.
20	boarding pass	A boarding pass is the pass that allows a passenger to get on the airplane.
21	boarding	Boarding is the process of passengers getting on an aircraft.
22	buckle	To buckle a seatbelt is to attach each side of the belt together. The buckled belt then forms a restraint.
23	cabin pressure	Cabin pressure is the amount of compressed oxygen pumped into an aircraft cabin to keep the passengers and crew safe and comfortable while flying.
24	cabin	A cabin is the part of an aircraft where passengers sit.
25	call button	A call button is a button located above passengers' seats that is used to notify flight attendants when passengers need help.
26	cargo forwarder	A cargo forwarder organizes the shipment of goods by plane to their final destination.
27	carry-on item	A carry-on item is an allowed bag or item that is carried with the passenger onto the airplane.
28	cart	A cart is a small-wheeled vehicle used to carry and transport snacks, trays, and drinks during a flight.
29	catering	Catering is the act of providing food and drinks for people at an event.
30	charter	A charter is an aircraft that is hired for the use of a select group of individuals.
31	chief purser	A chief purser is a senior flight attendant who oversees all flight attendants and pursers on board an aircraft.

32	cockpit	A cockpit is the front portion of an aircraft that houses the controls. It is where the pilots sit in order to operate an aircraft during a flight.
33	complimentary	If something is complimentary it is offered free of charge.
34	concourse	A concourse is part of a terminal, usually identified with a letter that contains a number of gates.
35	confirm	To confirm something is to make sure that it is true.
36	congestion	Congestion is the state of being overcrowded, especially with traffic or people.
37	connecting flight	A connecting flight is a flight in which passengers must stop and change planes or airlines before reaching their next destination.
38	connection	A connection is a flight that a passenger takes to continue on to his or her destination after getting off a previous flight.
39	CPR	CPR(cardiopulmonary resuscitation) involves compressing the chest and forcing air into the mouth in order to revive a stopped heartbeat or breathing.
40	crew change	A crew change is having a different set of staff on board to work.
41	crew resource management	Crew resource management(CRM) is a procedure designed to eliminate human error that may result in an accident.
42	customs	Customs is an agency that monitors goods that come in and go out of a country.
43	de-ice	To de-ice something is to remove ice (frozen water) from it.
44	delay	A delay means that the flight is slow or late to take off.
45	depart	To depart is to leave or exit.
46	deplane	To deplane is to leave an airplane.

47	descent	A descent is the lowering of height made by the aircraft.
48	destination	A destination is a place to which someone travels, or a place to which something is sent.
49	detect	To detect something is to find it.
50	disembark	To disembark is to leave an aircraft.
51	domestic	If something is domestic, it is within the boundaries of someone's own country.
52	electronic device	An electronic device is an instrument that depends on the flow of electricity to maintain its operation.
53	emergency equipment	Emergency equipment includes oxygen bottles, fire extinguishers, and other items that are used in a life-threatening situation.
54	en route	If something or someone is en route they are on their way someplace or in the midst of a journey.
55	estimated time of arrival	An estimated time of arrival(ETA) is the time at which a flight is scheduled to arrive someplace.
56	estimated time of departure	An estimated time of departure(ETD) is the time at which an airline is prepared for a flight to leave.
57	exit row	An exit row is a row of seats on an aircraft that is next to an emergency exit.
58	explosive detection	Explosive detection is an inspection process that determines whether something contains explosives.
59	fasten	The fasten something is to secure it, usually using two parts that attach together.
60	first aid kit	A first aid kit contains medical supplies that are used to give first-aid.
61	flight deck	A flight deck is the front protion of an aircraft that houses the controls. It is where the pilots sit in order to operate an aircraft during a flight.
62	flight dispatcher	A flight dispatcher plans and monitors flight routes to keep passengers and crew members safe.

63	flight number	A flight number is made up of an airline's name and three or four numbers which, when printed together, identify a particular flight.
64	flight time	Flight time is the total amount of time from when the plane first moves until the plane stops moving.
65	galley	A galley is an area on an aircraft where food and beverages are stored, jumpseats are located, and emergency equipment is stored.
66	ground time	Ground time is the amount of time an airplane spends on the ground between departure or arrival, taxiing, and parking at the gate.
67	identification	Identification is a card or a document that gives proof of who someone is.
68	impatient	If someone is impatient, he or she is unwilling to wait, or becomes bothered during moments of irritation, delay, or opposition.
69	in-flight entertainment	In-flight entertainment is comprised of the movies, music, and video games that are offered to passengers during a flight.
70	in-flight	If something occurs in-flight, it happens while a flight is in progress.
71	jumpseat	A jumpseat is folding seat on an aircraft that is used by crew members, usually located in a galley or flight deck.
72	land	To land is to bring an aircraft to the ground.
73	landing	A landing is when a plane makes contact with the ground after flight.
74	layover	A layover is a period of time in between flights.
75	life jacket	A life jacket is a personal flotation device used in emergency situations.
76	liquor	Liquor is any high-proof alcoholic drink.

77	local time	Local time is the current time in a city or country, including time zones.
78	lost-and-found	A lost-and-found is a place where personal belongings that have been forgotten are stored until their owners come to claim them.
79	narrow-body airliner	A narrow-body airliner is a small commercial aircraft that has one passenger aisle with seats on either side of the aisle.
80	overhead	If something is overhead, it means that it is directly above someone or something.
81	PA system	A PA system is a piece of equipment used for speaking to an audience in a space.
82	passenger head count	The passenger head count refers to the visual counting of passengers on the airplane.
83	passenger	A passenger is a person who travels on a plane.
84	post-flight	If something is post-flight, it refers to the time of inspection after the plane has landed and passengers have left the plane.
85	pre-flight	A pre-flight is the inspection and preparation of a aircraft before a flight departs.
86	regulation	A regulation is a rule that states how something must be done.
87	row	A row is a line of seats in an aircraft.
88	safety demonstration	A safety demonstration is a preflight explanation given to passengers about the safety features of an aircraft and how to use them.
89	secure	1) If something is secure it is safe, or not at risk of being lost or coming undone. 2) To secure something is to make sure that it is safe.
90	smoke detector	A smoke detector is used to discover the presence of smoke, indicating a fire

91	stand-by	To stand by is to wait for further information or instructions.
92	stock	To stock something is to supply it so it can be used in the future.
93	store	To store something is to put it away for later use.
94	stow	To stow something is to put or store it in a safe place for a period of time.
95	take-off	The take-off is when the plane leaves the ground.
96	taxiing	Taxiing refers to the plane slowly moving on the runway before take-off or after landing.
97	taxiway	A taxiway connects the different areas of a runway together.
98	terminal	A terminal is a building where passengers transfer on or off a planes.
99	tighten	To tighten something is to make it fit snugly around someone or something.
100	turbulence	Turbulence is instability of the atmosphere which can cause the airplane ride to be bumpy or unstable.
101	unaccompanied minor	An unaccompanied minor is a person under the age of 18 years old who is not with an adult.
102	upright	If a seat is upright it is sitting straight up. it is not reclined.
103	wide-body airliner	A wide-body airliner is a large commercial aircraft that has two passenger aisles with seats on either side of the aisles.
104	wing	A wing is one of two structures attached to the fuselage of an aircraft that create lift needed to fly.
105	wings	Wings are a badge that is worn by flight attendants and members of the flight crew. They are usually worn on the uniform jacket.

2. 국가별 출입국 서류

국가	여권	검역 설문서	입국 카드	세관 신고서	승무원 서류
대한민국	전 탑승객	해당 국가 작성 요함	전 외국인 작성	가족당 1부 작성	세관 신고서
중국	전 탑승객	비정상 상황에만 작성	전 외국인 (영어/중국어로 작성) 그룹 비자 소지 승객은 불필요함	유 · 소아 포함 1인당 1부 (영어/중국어로 작성) 세관품목 소지자만 작성	세관 신고서
일본	전 탑승객		전 외국인	가족당 1부	세관 신고서
미국	전 탑승객	세관 신고서에 검역 포함	전 외국인 (영어로 작성)	가족당 1부 작성 (검역 포함)	입국 카드/ 세관 신고서
영국	전 탑승객	별도로 없음	유럽 연합 외 국적 승객 작성 요함	별도로 없음	별도로 없음
타이	전 탑승객	별도로 없음	유 · 소아 포함 1인당 1부	구두 신고 가능	G/D 명단에 서명
호주	전 탑승객		arrival card (세관/검역 포함) 작성		aircrew- declaration 작성

3. First Aid Kit 내용품

의료 소모품

품목	수량
목록(list of kit contents)	1개
거즈(롤) 붕대(roller bandage)	4개
화상 처치용 거즈(burn gauze)	1개
바셀린 거즈(vaseline gauze)	1개
멸균 압박용 거즈(sterile compress gauze)	8개
멸균 거즈(sterile gauze)	1개
압박 붕대(bandage compresses)	8개
부목(splints for 16개 arm and leg)	2개
일회용 밴드(adhesive bandage compresses)	16개
삼각건, 안전핀(triangular bandage, safety pins)	5개
베타딘 스와프 또는 멸균 면봉(antiseptic swap)	20개
반창고(adhesive tape)	2개
상처 봉합용 테이프(sterile-strips)	1개
안대(pad with shield for eye)	1개
전자 체온계(thermometers (non-mercury))	1개
인공호흡을 위한 마스크-일방 통기 밸브용 (resuscitation mask with one-way valve)	1개
수술용 접착 테이프(adhesive surgical tape)	1개
일회용 의료 장갑(disposable gloves)	2개

손 세정제 또는 물수건(cleaning towelettes)	2개
가위(bandage scissors)	1개
핀셋(tweezers)	1개
사용 설명서(국문/영문) (the first aid manual)	1개
응급 처치 요령(the first aid manual)	1권
생존자용 지대공 시각 신호 코드 (ground air visual signal code for use by survivor)	1개

의약품

품목	수량
암모니아 흡입제(ammonia inhalants)	10개
타이레놀 혹은 기타 해열 진통제(analgesics, antipyretics)	5정
보나링 A 혹은 기타 멀미약(motion sickness medication)	5정
부스코판 또는 기타 진경제(antispasmodics)	5정
나리스타-S 혹은 기타 점비액(decongestant nasal spray)	1개
페니라민 또는 항히스타민제(antihistamines)	5정
겔포스 또는 제산제(anti-acids)	1포
정로환 또는 지사제(antidiarrheic agent)	12정

4. Emergency Medical Kit

의료 장비

내용품 목록(list of contents)	가이드북(reference guide)
청진기(stethoscope)	혈압계(sphygmomanometer)
항균 소독포 (alchol sponge, povidone iodine swabstick)	일회용 주사기 및 주삿바늘 (disposable syringes and needles)
인공 기도(airway)	정맥 주사용 카테터(IV catheter)
일회용 의료 장갑(surgical glove)	지혈대(tourniquet)
도뇨관(foley catheter)	수액 세트
스펀지 거즈(sterilized gauze sponge)	주삿바늘 폐기함(needle disposable box)
접착 테이프(tape)	외과용 마스크(surgical mask)
기관 카테터(endotracheal tube)	탯줄 집게(umbilical cord clamp)
전자 체온계(electronic thermometer)	인공 호흡용 백 마스크(bag valve mask)
기본 인명 구조술 지침서 (basic life support card)	손전등과 건전지(illuminator)

의약품

아드레날린제 또는 에피네프린(epinephrine)	기관지 확장제 – 흡입식(bronchodilator)
항히스타민제 – 주사용(antihistamine)	아트로핀(atropine sulfate)
정맥 주사용 포도당(50% dextrose)	부신 피질 스테로이드 주사제(hydrocortisone)
나이트로글리세린 정제(nitrostat)	이뇨제 – 주사용(diuretics)
진통제(analgesics)	자궁 수축제(uterotonic agent)
항경련제 – 주사용(sedatives)	경구용 베타 수용제 차단제(beta blocker)
진토제 – 주사용(antiemetic)	아스피린 – 경구용(aspirin)
주사용 생리 식염수(intravenous & other sterile solutions)	

Tongue Twisters

Please try talking a turn on these
tongue-tangling twisters.

♬

A skunk sat on a stump and thunk the stump stunk,
but the stump thunk the skunk stunk.

♬

A big black bug bit a big black bear,
made the big bear bleed blood.

♬

One smart fellow, he felt smart.

Two smart fellows, they felt smart.

Three smart fellows, they all felt smart.

She sells sea shells by the sea shore.

The shells she sells are surely seashells.

So if she sells shells on the shore, I'm sure she sells seashore shells.

♬

A flea and a fly flew up in a flue.

Said the flea, "Let us fly!"

Said the fly, "Let us flee!"

So they through a flaw in the future.

저자 약력

이효선

Concordia University. BA. Human Relations 전공
중앙대학교 인적자원개발학 석사
중앙대학교 인적자원개발학 박사
Canada College TESOL Certificate 과정 이수
전) 대한항공 객실승무부 부사무장
대한항공 객실훈련원 강사
일본 CAJ International School English Instructor
현) 극동대학교 항공운항서비스학과 교수

이진영

배재대학교 컨설팅학 석사
배재대학교 컨설팅학 박사
Oxford Seminars TESOL Certificate 과정 이수
전) 대한항공 객실승무부 국제선 승무원
현) 극동대학교 항공운항서비스학과 외래교수
사단법인 한국외식산업학회 부회장
사단법인 한국외식산업학회 편집부원장